# The 3000 Questions About Myself Book for Her

# The 3000 Questions About Myself Book for Her

A Questions About Me Book for Her, Filled With Thoughtful Prompts for Self-Reflection, Emotional Clarity, and Connection

Aria Capri Publishing Group
Mauricio Vasquez
Toronto, Canada

Authors:
Aria Capri Publishing Group
Mauricio Vasquez
First Printing: May 2025

ISBN 978-1-998729-49-4 (Electronic book)
ISBN 978-1-998729-48-7 (Hardcover book)
ISBN 978-1-998729-47-0 (Paperback)

## Introduction

There's something sacred about a woman's decision to turn inward and truly ask herself, *"How am I, really?"* That quiet moment of self-inquiry is more than reflection—it is an act of courage, a declaration of worth, and a return to self. In a world that often demands our attention, our energy, and our caretaking, taking the time to listen to your own heart is nothing short of revolutionary.

This book was created with you in mind—with your emotional depth, your longing for clarity, your capacity for connection, and your quiet wisdom. This book isn't just a collection of prompts. It's a gentle companion, a mirror, and a doorway into deeper knowing. Whether you're seeking grounding in your daily life, healing from life's aches, or simply longing to feel more connected—to yourself and to those you love—these questions are here to guide you.

We produced this book because we believe women deserve more moments of stillness and self-recognition. We are often so focused on supporting others that we forget how powerful it can be to pause and ask ourselves meaningful questions. What do I truly want? What part of me needs tenderness? What dream have I tucked away?

You don't need a perfect morning routine or a silent retreat to begin. Just a few minutes and a willingness to show up honestly.

There are many ways to use this book:

- In solitude, as a daily reflection practice—whether in the quiet of the morning, during a mindful walk, or before bed.
- With a friend, over tea or text, as a way to deepen your bond through real, vulnerable conversations.
- With a partner, using these prompts to foster intimacy and emotional connection in your relationship.
- In group settings, such as women's circles, coaching sessions, or retreats, where shared truth creates powerful resonance.

The questions inside touch on every layer of your being—from playful curiosity to deep emotional truths. Some will make you smile, others may stir tears or spark long-buried desires. All are invitations to return to yourself.

You don't need to answer every question. Let your intuition lead. What matters is that you show up—not perfectly, but honestly. This is your space. Your pace. Your story.

And through this journey, you may just find what's been waiting within you all along: clarity, confidence, and a more loving relationship with yourself.

Welcome to your next chapter. Let's begin—one soulful question at a time.

## How to Use This Book

- **Follow your instinct.** Each question is a gentle prompt—choose what speaks to you in the moment. There's no need to overthink; the magic is in the honesty, not the perfection.

- **Let your answers lead you.** Go beyond a quick response. Ask yourself *why*—that's where clarity, healing, and true insight begin.

- **Move in your own rhythm.** Start at the beginning or open to a page that draws you in. Reflect silently, speak your truth out loud, or write your thoughts in a journal—it's all welcome here.

- **There are no wrong answers.** This is your safe space. Be real. Be tender. Be unfiltered. Every part of you belongs.

- **Create space for reflection.** Set aside a quiet moment. Silence the noise. Let this time be a gift you give to yourself—or someone you love.

- **Follow the conversation.** If a question takes you somewhere unexpected, go with it. Some of the most meaningful discoveries are found off-script.

- **Let it feel good.** These prompts are here to support you—not just in growth, but in joy, connection, and moments of soulful lightness.

## A Quick Favor to Ask

If this book has inspired reflection, sparked meaningful conversations, or brought you closer to someone in your life, I'd be incredibly grateful if you could take a moment to leave a review.

As an independent author without the resources of a big publishing house, your feedback truly makes a difference. Reviews help others discover this book, and they remind me why this work matters—one question, one reader at a time.

To share your thoughts, simply scan the QR code. It only takes a minute, but your words will go a long way.

Thank you, sincerely, for your time and support

Aria Capri Publishing

**P.S. Don't miss your free bonus!**

You'll find a special gift waiting for you at the **end of this book**—a digital version of *THIS IS MY WAY* you can download and keep with you wherever you go.

# Keep Growing, Keep Asking:
## Discover More Titles

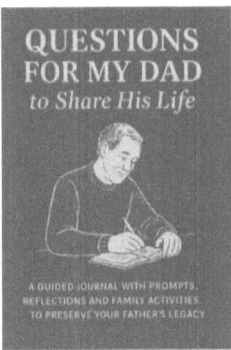

## The 3000 Questions About Myself Book for Her

1. What recent moment made you stop and say, "Wow, I never thought of it that way before"?

2. Would you ever want someone to tell you your future, even if it meant hearing something emotional or unexpected?

3. What meaningful action or success would make your coworkers want to clap for you?

4. What did you last look up that made you feel more informed, inspired, or even amused?

5. When was the last time you gave yourself a break, stayed in your pajamas, and just took care of your soul?

6. Which gemstone reflects your inner sparkle — your resilience, grace, or spirit?

7. What animal story touched your heart because of the courage, loyalty, or love it showed?

8. What season feels most like "home" to you — comforting, beautiful, or emotionally rich?

9. Tell me about a Monday that started with stress but taught you something about your strength.

10. How do you balance being a trustworthy friend with doing what feels morally right?

11. What item would leave you scrambling if it disappeared overnight — practical or sentimental?

12. What's something on your heart or list that you've been avoiding — but know it's time to face?

13. Was there a moment when something playful turned into a mess — how did you feel about it afterward?

14. What daily task drains your energy — and how amazing would it feel to let it go for good?

15. What timeless song touches your soul, even though it came out before you were born?

16. Is there something playful or superstitious you still do, even if it makes no logical sense?

17. What uplifting or empowering messages would you want someone to read in their next fortune cookie?

18. What two movies — maybe with very different vibes — would be wildly entertaining if their stars switched?

19. What part of your personality, presence, or heart do people most often appreciate out loud?

20. How do you feel about second chances for people sentenced to life in prison? Should time or change matter?

21. What TV character from your younger years still holds a special place in your heart?

22. What unusual or little-known moment from history has always captured your imagination?

23. What did you do today that was kind, brave, or strong — even if it felt ordinary?

24. If you had a quiet bench to remember your life, where would it sit — in nature, in a city, or somewhere personal?

25. If your go-to username was a perfume, what kind of fragrance would capture your personality or mood?

26. If your face could send a message or spark change, what kind of beauty or strength would it show?
27. Which version of James Bond felt the most exciting, stylish, or emotionally interesting to watch?
28. What challenge did you rise to, especially when others underestimated you?
29. If a glass had a new name that sounded elegant, fun, or cozy, what would you call it?
30. What choices or mindset shifts would you bring into high school if you had a second chance?
31. What's something you recently did that felt like a deep exhale — something you've needed to do for ages?
32. Who would be your dream duet partner, and what emotional or empowering song would you choose to sing?
33. Who's someone you quietly miss — and what would reconnecting with them mean to you now?
34. What hair or beauty items make you feel your most confident, centered, or radiant self?
35. What three colors express your energy, mood, and inner beauty the best?
36. If animals could talk, which one would sound the most dramatic or emotional — and why?
37. What's the one candy you'd be excited to steal from your kids' trick-or-treat bag?
38. What's a soft, clever, or unexpectedly funny "mom joke" that would make everyone roll their eyes and smile?
39. Have you ever learned how to tie different knots — and if so, what's your favorite one and why?

40. What animal without a tail would look hilariously fabulous or uniquely graceful if it suddenly had one?

41. What's an embarrassing moment that made you blush but also taught you something about confidence?

42. What's your go-to move when a telemarketer calls — do you feel guilty hanging up?

43. What name do you feel connected to, even if it's not the one you were given at birth?

44. When was the last time you dipped into the sea — was it freeing, healing, or just plain fun?

45. What job's outfit do you secretly love — for the confidence, the flair, or the tradition it brings?

46. Have you ever had a life-altering moment that started with someone you didn't expect to meet?

47. What's a moment when your smile betrayed you — thanks to a very uninvited snack?

48. A box of puppies shows up at your door — how do you handle the adorable chaos?

49. What word makes you cringe or feel small — one you'd love to never hear again?

50. What karaoke song do you love to sing — the one that lets you shine or laugh freely?

51. Would you consider easing your child's grief by offering comfort through a gentle cover-up?

52. Do you think something wiser or more evolved exists in the universe — and how does that idea sit with your heart?

53. Are there friendships from your childhood you've carried into adulthood? What do they mean to you now?

54. What magical or hopeful idea from childhood do you wish still felt real to you?

55. If you could bless a baby you've never met, what gift would carry your love and hope for their future?

56. What kind of brilliance do you recognize most — emotional, creative, or intellectual?

57. There's water dripping — what's the fastest way you'd react, even in the middle of a busy day?

58. Where would you escape to in an instant if you had the power to go anywhere — for beauty, healing, or joy?

59. If you could rewrite that old saying about waiting, what lighthearted or cozy version would you use?

60. Have you ever danced, stretched, or sweat your way through a fitness video at home? Which one was your favorite?

61. If you could rename the fly, what quirky or lighthearted word would you come up with?

62. What gave you a shock recently — and did it make you laugh, jump, or groan?

63. How did you find answers or explore curiosities before search engines existed?

64. What noises overwhelm your nervous system or disturb your peace more than others?

65. If your workspace could overlook any scene, what would calm or energize you most?

66. What cute or whimsical animals would you love to see in a box of crackers — and what would they taste like?

67. What dream restaurant would you visit to review — maybe for the comfort, ambiance, or a favorite dish?

68. What font feels expressive or elegant to you — the one you secretly hope people notice?

69. Have you ever done something playful like sliding down a bannister — when was the last time?

70. Imagine a joyful balloon explosion — how many could you fill your space with, just for fun?

71. If you gave yourself permission to spend money today just for pleasure, what would you pick up?

72. When was the last time you dipped your feet into something relaxing, new, or symbolic?

73. When did you last feel moved to connect with a stranger, and what did you share or learn?

74. What filmmaker would understand your emotional depth, humor, and challenges well enough to tell your story?

75. Is there a movie that everyone raved about but left you wondering what the fuss was about?

76. What small charm or keychain has stayed with you — and what memory or meaning does it carry?

77. What famous athlete comes to mind when you think of global recognition and impact?

78. Is there a day from your past you'd love to return to — for the joy, meaning, or beauty it held?

79. Were you ever caught in a white lie or big one — and what was the lesson in that moment?

80. What do you remember about the last rainbow you saw — the timing, the sky, or your emotions?

81. What emotional or symbolic color would you assign to a rainstorm — and what name would you call it?

82. Is there something you hold close to your heart, that brings comfort or meaning — your own "precious"?

83. Which costume party look made you feel fun, bold, or completely in character?

84. What would your modern magic style be — what would take the place of a cauldron, cloak, or cat?

85. Could you imagine giving up your dominant thumb in exchange for perfect health — would you say yes?

86. What's your must-have Monopoly property — the one you feel lucky or powerful owning?

87. How would you invest a surprise amount of money in a way that reflects your values and dreams?

88. What's a memorable or delightful item you found on eBay — something that brought joy or solved a problem?

89. What's a non-verbal way of connecting or expressing that you find beautiful or unusual?

90. If you could take a carefree day for joy, peace, or inspiration, where would you go?

91. If you could talk with any animal heart-to-heart, which one would you choose and why?

92. What would help you find peace in choosing the right time to say goodbye to a cherished pet?

93. What city, state, or country name sounds funny or fabulous enough to be a celebrity baby's name?

94. When you're on a long flight, what kind of seat feels most comfortable, peaceful, or exciting to you?

95. What task have you rushed through for fun, pride, or just to prove something to yourself?

96. In a moment of unexpected messiness, how do you handle being seen without losing grace?

97. What carnival ride gives you butterflies in the best way — or just makes you feel alive?

98. When you're stuck far from help and out of options, what instincts kick in to get you through?

99. What long book felt like a real journey — and what part of it still stays with you?

100. If you were a magical being, where would you quietly wait to help others — and how would they summon you?

101. What word best reflects the heart of your closest friend — strength, warmth, or light?

102. Do you think traffic-free zones in cities would make them feel safer, cleaner, or more inviting?

103. When was the last time you realized something could've gone badly but didn't — and how did it feel?

104. Have you ever gone quiet and hidden when someone came to your door? What made you do it?

105. What imaginative or helpful things would you want in place of hands if you lived in a magical world?
106. What three personal or beautiful things remind you most of your favorite color?
107. Would you say yes if someone asked for a paid selfie — or would you trust your instincts and decline?
108. What truth, no matter how difficult, opened your eyes and made you stronger?
109. Do you know the names of the people living closest to you — and have you shared more than a hello?
110. Did a school report ever say something about you that you challenged by becoming your truest self?
111. What competitive activity do you think is fun but maybe doesn't belong in the sports category?
112. With a surprise afternoon off, what's something peaceful, energizing, or creative you'd do just for you?
113. Have you ever sipped or bitten into something you thought was delicious — and it turned out awful?
114. What actress or actor feels like they're just being themselves in every role they take on?
115. What qualities — grace, resilience, heart — turn a person into someone unforgettable?
116. What subject area do you shine in when trivia games come out — books, people, or moments in time?
117. If you could return to your younger self and make a choice, would college still be part of your story?

118. What's a misspelled tattoo you've seen or heard of that made you feel secondhand embarrassment?

119. If every step had to be forward — no turning back — what would you rethink or do differently today?

120. Have you ever had an awkward moment like drooling in public — and how did you laugh it off?

121. Would you choose sisters for the bond, brothers for the play, or mix it up for fun and balance?

122. Could you imagine letting go of one year to give your beloved animal another year of comfort and love?

123. What bird imitation made you laugh, pause, or wonder how they learn to mimic us so well?

124. What's your guess for how many gummy bears could fit in your mouth — and would you try it?

125. Which charity speaks to your heart — where your time and care could make a real difference?

126. What's a playful or lighthearted expression you use to describe someone who's a bit clueless at times?

127. When was the last time you scrolled through someone's posts to get a feel for who they are?

128. When have you asked someone for something really important — and what did that moment teach you?

129. Have you met someone who shares your last name but isn't family? What was that moment like for you?

130. If a gentle stray followed you home, would your heart tell you to care for it, or seek another way to help?

131. Before you drift off, what three things from today brought you warmth, pride, or peace?

132. How would you handle an unexpected silence before an interview — with patience, confidence, or curiosity?

133. What prank have you pulled that was funny but kind-hearted — and how did they react?

134. If a free vacation dropped into your lap but you had to decide instantly, what place would call your name?

135. What weight or health goal would feel most empowering and loving for your body and mind?

136. What Sesame Street friend made you feel happy, safe, or inspired — and why did they stand out?

137. Is there a frenemy or rival who challenged you — and maybe even helped you grow?

138. When did you last exchange a smile with a stranger — maybe in a grocery store, park, or coffee shop?

139. Which decade holds the most beauty or inspiration for you — in style, values, or dreams?

140. If today's emotions were a song, what melody or artist would best capture your story?

141. Which high school love stories have you seen that grew into real, enduring partnerships?

142. Is there a guilty pleasure food that makes you pay the price with gas or an upset stomach afterward?

143. Have you ever played a role-playing game like Dungeons and Dragons — or would you love to try it someday?

144. Can you remember a time when worry or frustration blew something small way out of proportion?

145. What changes or losses might break the heart of someone traveling from 50 years ago to now?

146. What quiet moments of solitude do you cherish — and how do they feed your spirit?

147. Have you ever tried something super trendy that left you thinking, "Was that it?"

148. Where do you think your food choices fall between indulgence and nourishment?

149. If you could name the next wave of kids growing up today, what would you call their generation?

150. If you could exchange some years for a fortune, would you do it — and what would matter more, time or money?

151. If you could choose six people to keep you strong, safe, and smiling on a deserted island, who would they be?

152. Was there ever a moment you found your way into somewhere without a ticket — and how did it make you feel?

153. If aliens trusted you to show them the heart of humanity, where would you take them first?

154. What singing duos — blending male and female voices — do you love most for their harmony or chemistry?

155. What foods, sweet or savory, would you love to taste with a delicious coat of chocolate?

156. Imagine you're invincible and falling from the sky — what funny, stylish, or wild way would you land?

157. What cute, dramatic, or funny way do you like to say, "I'm soooo tired"?

158. Would you ever stop to help a stranger on the side of the road — and what would guide your decision?

159. What spirit animal feels like it captures your soul — strength, intuition, beauty, or freedom?

160. If you could adjust your height with magic, would you grow taller, get smaller, or love yourself just as you are?

161. Do you find comfort in moving through stores the same way, or do you explore with no set path?

162. Which award from your childhood reminds you of your first taste of hard-earned pride?

163. How would you want future generations to speak about your kindness, courage, or creativity?

164. Who in sports history do you think hurt the spirit of competition by cheating?

165. Who would be hilariously wrong to cast as Indiana Jones — and why would it be so funny?

166. If you had to pick a specialty to show your brilliance, what topic would you feel most confident about?

167. When you hear "nerd," what qualities come to mind — and do you see them as beautiful or bold?

168. Have you ever booked a hotel that looked dreamy online but felt totally disappointing in person?

169. If you witnessed a coworker taking something they shouldn't, what would your heart and conscience tell you to do?

170. When was the last time you shared a bath — was it romantic, playful, or just a simple memory?

171. What kinds of moments pull you toward protecting yourself first — and when has it mattered most?

172. If you had to pick a word that would cause chaos just by shouting it, what would you choose?

173. What would be loaded on your dream ship — love, adventure, wisdom, or peace?

174. Before you drift off at night, what little routine or comforting thought always comes first?

175. If you could whisk someone away on a cruise, who would you bring along to laugh, relax, and explore with?

176. What kind of chaotic, funny, or powerful result would happen if every human jumped at the same time?

177. Have you ever wondered what all those extra buttons do — or do you have a few trusty ones you always use?

178. Which cozy, stylish shade of beige feels most like you — and what whimsical name would you give it?

179. If you could invent a name for a brave, bold new Musketeer, what would it sound like?

180. When was the last time you shared a bath — was it romantic, playful, or just a simple memory?

181. What kinds of moments pull you toward protecting yourself first — and when has it mattered most?

182. If you had to pick a word that would cause chaos just by shouting it, what would you choose?

183. What would be loaded on your dream ship — love, adventure, wisdom, or peace?

184. Before you drift off at night, what little routine or comforting thought always comes first?

185. If you could whisk someone away on a cruise, who would you bring along to laugh, relax, and explore with?

186. What kind of chaotic, funny, or powerful result would happen if every human jumped at the same time?

187. Have you ever wondered what all those extra buttons do — or do you have a few trusty ones you always use?

188. Which cozy, stylish shade of beige feels most like you — and what whimsical name would you give it?

189. If you could invent a name for a brave, bold new Musketeer, what would it sound like?

190. Would seeing breakdancing at the Olympics excite you — celebrating creativity and strength together?

191. What's a scientific name you find weird, wonderful, or even a little silly?

192. Can you remember a moment when you thought, "Am I really doing this?" What happened?

193. What funny, sweet, or surprising "most likely to..." labels would fit three of your friends?

194. What subject would you love to learn deeply about — something that would open up new worlds for you?

195. What's your most cringe-worthy moment inside a fitting room?

196. If you were a mischievous spirit, who would you choose to gently spook for fun?

197. Where do you wish you could slow down and give more presence or care in your daily life?

198. In another universe, what magical or mysterious things could be going on at Area 51?

199. Could you see yourself cutting it all off to raise money for something close to your heart?

200. Do old superstitions like ladders and black cats make you more cautious — or do you shrug them off?

201. What's the scariest storm you've lived through — and what helped you feel safe in the middle of it?

202. What three fun, delicious treats would you pack for a cozy or adventurous picnic?

203. Would you follow a dream job if money didn't matter — or would you stay where you feel strongest?

204. Can you think of a small accident that caused you a lot of pain but now makes for a funny story?

205. Has there ever been a time you helped a friend, partner, or sibling pop a pimple? How did it feel?

206. When did you last scream — whether in excitement, surprise, or absolute panic?

207. If you had to choose, what surprising ordinary thing would be the one way to defeat your immortal hero?

208. What's a task you think feels too overwhelming or lonely to do without someone by your side?

209. What national parks have you visited that made you feel small, awed, or wonderfully alive?

210. How do you like to safeguard your files, memories, or work — and why does that method work for you?

211. If Alice wandered into a new dream world, who might she meet — someone kind, strange, or magical?

212. When did you first experience that quiet, serious feeling that you had truly grown up?

213. If you could customize your ride for joy, safety, or style, what would you add to it?

214. Do you believe that passion, vision, or heart can make someone indispensable in a workplace?

215. When you're home alone, what unfamiliar or creepy sound would instantly make you nervous?

216. Have you had a cozy night sleeping in a sleeping bag — outdoors, at a sleepover, or somewhere unexpected?

217. Is there a smell — food, perfume, or nature — that you just can't stand even for a second?

218. If you were turned into a magical giant garden gnome, what happy, silly, or graceful pose would you take?

219. In the Scooby-Doo gang, who do you feel you're most like — Daphne's heart, Velma's brains, or another?

220. How would your friends rate your dance moves — shy two-stepper, freestyle queen, or hidden talent?

221. How many of your online friends are real-life companions you still laugh, talk, and connect with regularly?

222. What's the small essential you carry everywhere for peace of mind — even if you rarely need it?

223. If you magically swapped places with the lead in the last show you watched, who would you be today?

224. Which Disney movie still makes you smile, sing, or cry — or what's your reason for not having a favorite?

225. If leadership found you, what group or cause would you proudly take charge of?

226. What dairy-free milk option feels best to you — for taste, health, or lifestyle?

227. Which pie would win your heart at Thanksgiving — a savory favorite or a sweet treat you can't resist?

228. What new type of personal device do you dream of seeing next — small, smart, or super creative?

229. Can you ever fully forgive someone without letting part of the memory stay with you for protection?

230. If every country joined together, what city would you want to be the heart of this new world?

231. What's a memory of tough physical work that made you stronger, proud, or more determined?

232. Would you be open to trying squirrel meat if it meant embracing new experiences?

233. Would you go for the glamorous car or the practical cash if the decision was yours alone?

234. How many hours a week do you unwind in front of the TV — and do you ever wish it was less or more?

235. Have you ever had the joy of wearing another country's traditional clothes — and how did it feel?

236. What three wishes do you think your best friend would make if magic was real today?

237. What's the most calorie-packed food you'd bring on a long hike to stay strong and energized?

238. Would any amount of money tempt you to gain a hundred pounds for a year — or is health worth more?

239. What herb, spice, or seasoning do you quietly leave out when following a recipe — and why?

240. Have you ever sat on something small and unpleasant by accident — what happened next?

241. If you were blindfolded and picked your destination by accident, what place would you hope not to land on?

242. What's the last fun, unusual, or smart-sounding word you learned, and where did you hear it?

243. If you made a family coat of arms, what symbols of strength, love, or creativity would you add?

244. Have you ever seen something in slow motion that felt magical, emotional, or completely unforgettable?

245. Are there actors you admire but wish could show a wider range than the parts they always seem to get?

246. What breakfast ingredients make you happiest — something simple, sweet, cozy, or bold?

247. If you were an insect for a day, what would you be — colorful like a butterfly, busy like a bee?

248. What clothing choice would you dread explaining if you ended up in a hospital emergency room?

249. How many accounts do you follow on social media — and how do you decide who stays or goes?

250. What sweet, dreamy cotton candy flavor would you design to make everyone's day sweeter?

251. Have you enjoyed a playful ride on a seesaw recently — and what made it memorable?

252. What tradition from another place left you feeling amazed, curious, or a little puzzled?

253. How would you turn a sudden blackout into a cozy, calm, or even adventurous night?

254. When do you allow "good enough" — and when do you hold out for something greater?

255. What three fruits, flavors, or add-ins would you pick to craft your dream smoothie?

256. What meal or treat is so tasty you just can't help licking your fingers afterward?

257. Which music festival feels like your perfect dream — relaxing vibes, electric energy, or deep soul?

258. If you ruled the diving board, what graceful or dramatic dive would you invent — and what would you call it?

259. Which sci-fi movie do you think captures what our world could truly become — for better or worse?

260. What modern gadget would you transform into a whimsical, vintage-looking steampunk masterpiece?

261. Who's the last person you played frisbee with — and was it a fun, silly, or memorable game?

262. Which cookie-and-milk combination feels like pure comfort to you — crunchy, gooey, or chocolatey?

263. If today's thoughts popped up in the air above you, would you be laughing, hiding, or saying "oops"?

264. Which cute or cringey childhood memory does your family love to tell to tease you a little?

265. Have you ever felt a silence so deep that it made you feel small, peaceful, or maybe even uneasy?

266. What's your final "just to be safe" step before locking the door and heading away for a few days?

267. If you could change your birthday to a new day that felt more "you," what would it be and why?

268. What treasured toy from when you were small still lives with you — tucked in a memory box or on a shelf?

269. If you had to get out of a flooded underground tunnel with just your wits, what would you grab and do?

270. What's the most hilariously awkward name you've heard — real or made up?

271. When it comes to expiration dates, are you flexible or do you prefer to play it safe with food?

272. How would you react if you spilled red wine on a white carpet — quick thinking or quiet regret?

273. If you had a magic wand, what one word would you say to make amazing things happen?

274. If you could make a wild movie with something silly or scary on a plane, what would you pick?

275. If your last meal became a masterpiece on display, what playful or emotional name would you give it?

276. What's the funniest or weirdest face you've noticed hidden in an object — and who did it remind you of?

277. If you gave Velma, Daphne, and Fred trendy, fresh names today, what would you pick for them?

278. Do you remember the excitement (or mystery) of the tooth fairy visiting you as a child?

279. What life experience caught you by surprise — something you never dared imagine could happen?

280. When did you last gift yourself a moment of pure silence — and what did you notice inside yourself?

281. If you had to rename Alvin the chipmunk, what cute or sassy new name would you choose?

282. If you spent a day without one of your senses, which would you choose — and how would it change your experience?

283. What one-player game fills your spirit — maybe a puzzle, a solo card game, or something creative?

284. Did you ever look at someone's journal or diary — even just a little — and what did you learn?

285. What's the last non-selfie picture you snapped — something that caught your heart or your eye?

286. If you could wake up tomorrow a master at something, what empowering or joyful talent would you pick?

287. What's your most vivid piñata memory — joyful, silly, or surprisingly intense?

288. Would you rather see Christmas magic arrive only in December, or do you love seeing it early?

289. Is there a little thing you keep forgetting — appointments, keys, birthdays — that drives you crazy?

290. How many hugs do you share on an average day — and what do they mean to you emotionally?

291. If you had to rename the orange without using its color, what sweet or playful name would you give it?

292. Is there something comforting to you about drinking iced coffee or tea even on a cold winter day?

293. Do you have a favorite Clint Eastwood movie that resonates with you — or does he not make your list?

294. If you could express yourself through painting landscapes, what place would inspire you most?

295. What amazing or inspiring thing have you seen people do using their feet when hands weren't an option?

296. Which room in your house feels like your happy place — cozy, lively, or peaceful?

297. If you could limit one day to appearing once every four years, what day would you happily see less often?

298. Which three musicians or performers would you wish to magically see share a stage for one unforgettable show?

299. If your everyday knowledge could instantly earn you a PhD, what would your field of expertise be?

300. Have you ever seen a gorgeous-looking dish that turned out to taste nothing like you hoped?

301. Have you ever brought a store-bought cake to a party and let people think you baked it?

302. What new, cute, or clever item would you put on a rope if you were launching a new trend?

303. What face do you make that clearly shows your feelings, even if you stay completely silent?

304. If you turned your name into an acronym, what inspiring or creative words would each letter represent?

305. Where would it be absolutely terrifying or heartbreaking to experience a medical emergency alone?

306. Which color brings back memories of holidays for you — warmth, sparkle, or tradition?

307. Have you ever done a "just-in-case" stockpile run — filling your shelves with food or home goods?

308. If pandas were colorful like rainbows, what fun or beautiful colors would you pick for them?

309. If you could craft something gigantic visible from space, what inspiring or artistic thing would you create?

310. In your opinion, what ingredient truly loses its magic when it's canned or frozen?

311. Do you believe anything is possible if you dream big — or are there things you think just can't happen?

312. Would you ever eat a beetle for fun, for a dare, or just to surprise people?

313. If Hansel and Gretel were modern kids, what would they leave behind instead of bread crumbs?

314. What flavors would you blend to create a delicious, refreshing ice cream float masterpiece?

315. What's a memory of heartbreak that still lingers — and what strength did you find afterward?

316. What's one habit — big or small — that you find the most annoying to deal with?

317. What was the last time something unfair or frustrating made you wonder, "Why me?"

318. If a fluffy bunny's fate depended on it, could you say the alphabet backwards in 30 seconds?

319. If you had to make up a silly but convincing excuse for being late, what would you say?

320. Have you seen or experienced a long-distance relationship that thrived — and what helped it?

321. If you had a magical edible plate, what flavor would make every meal feel even more special?

322. If you forgot your packed lunch, how would you solve the lunchtime crisis — creatively or simply?

323. Which color seems to have lost its trendiness — but still holds a place in your wardrobe?

324. Besides lemonade, what delicious treat or dish do you love using lemons for?

325. Is there a Christmas carol you secretly (or openly) wish you didn't have to hear again?

326. If you had to compete tomorrow for your country, what sport would you be best (or least bad) at?

327. What past argument feels pointless now — something you realize didn't really matter at all?

328. What ravioli filling brings you the most comfort or makes you the happiest?

329. What sound reminds you of long summer days — laughter, waves, music, or something else?

330. Was there a moment when a tiny act of kindness made your whole day — or even changed your outlook?

331. What's the last command or curious question you asked your smart speaker at home?

332. What treasures — fresh, homemade, or colorful — do you love finding at a farmers market?

333. What first job helps teenagers build confidence, skills, and a sense of pride?

334. What three words capture your day's energy or vibe so far?

335. If you could wallow in something just for the joy of it, what cozy or fabulous thing would it be?

336. If asked to speak about your workplace on TV, would you jump in proudly or tread carefully?

337. What imaginative or artistic thing could you build using only old newspapers?

338. When you need support, comfort, or wisdom, who's the first person you turn to?

339. Which ancient landmark feels too precious to ever lose — a symbol of beauty, strength, or history?

340. If you could share one piece of good or historic news as a news anchor, what story would it be?

341. What new, empowering, or unexpected ending would you give Little Red Riding Hood?

342. Do you believe that angels walk among us — or that you might have seen or felt one near you?

343. What leftover foods would make a pie so bad you couldn't even pretend to be polite?

344. What nickname would your closest friends invent for you that captures your spirit or energy?

345. If you could keep one magical or legendary item from a movie, what would you pick?

346. Have you ever felt so full after a meal that you had to lie down for a while?

347. What three happy moments, memories, or hopes are lifting your heart today?

348. How many friends, coworkers, or classmates have the same first name as you — and is it fun or confusing?

349. What's the last thing that made you smile, pause, and say, "That's cool!" — even in your head?

350. Which magical creature would you love to know really existed — and how would it change the world?

351. What cozy, exciting, or delicious spot would you recommend to visitors looking for a meal in your town?

352. Would you dare to taste unknown food — trusting your senses — and have you tried before?

353. What's the oddest, creepiest, or most fascinating cult you've heard of?

354. What nonverbal way would you use to let someone know you were upset without speaking?

355. Is your home full of 24-hour digital clocks, or do you like the old-fashioned way better?

356. Have you ever had a funny moment when something labeled "easy" ended up being anything but?

357. What type of frosting makes every cake taste even better in your opinion?

358. When did you last throw caution to the wind and dance, sing, or laugh the night away?

359. What's the most beautiful tiny thing you've ever seen in nature — a bug, flower, or something else?

360. If you invented a miracle super glue, what powerful or stylish name would you pick?

361. If you reinvented Butch Cassidy and the Sundance Kid, what adventurous or clever names would you choose?

362. If you could erase a household chore from your list with a snap, which one would you love to ditch?

363. What scents make you feel cozy, peaceful, or at home — lavender, cookies, ocean air?

364. If your life events inspired a film title based on weddings and funerals attended, what would it be?

365. What character from a children's tale scared you when you were small, even if you laugh about it now?

366. How would you rewrite the "Twelve Days of Christmas" with today's trends and surprises?

367. Which radio station or music app do you love most for setting your daily vibe?

368. Growing up (or even now), did you or your family use funny or cute nicknames for body parts?

369. How far would you chase your runaway umbrella before deciding it just wasn't worth it anymore?

370. How many fries would you consider a fair trade for giving up a delicious chicken nugget?

371. Which famous person looks even more fabulous now that they've gotten older?

372. If baboons had fashionable bottoms in a new color, what vibrant shade would you pick?

373. What's your funniest or most frustrating story about struggling with "easy open" packaging?

374. Was there something that recently made you scratch like crazy — a sweater, grass, or something else?

375. What pie would win the crown as your ultimate favorite if you made a top ten list?

376. What makes a wedding outfit not just beautiful but truly meaningful or stylish in your eyes?

377. Do you believe everyone has a secret look-alike somewhere — and have you spotted yours yet?

378. When you forget what something's called, what silly substitute word do you like to use?

379. Do you believe it's more honorable to return ancient remains to their origins instead of keeping them on display?

380. If gum came in savory flavors, what yummy taste would you love — cheesy, herby, or something else?

381. Have you ever stumbled on a headstone that made you pause, reflect, or even cry a little?

382. When did you last have a moment so disappointing that all you could say was, "That sucks"?

383. Have you ever played a really unusual sport — and what made it so different or hilarious?

384. Which three photos on your phone are too precious to delete, no matter what?

385. Which three songs are your guilty pleasures for singing your heart out in the shower?

386. What was the last podcast you got totally hooked on — and what was it about?

387. What's your go-to playlist when you're determined to finish something — strong, sassy, or bold tracks?

388. How would you describe your hard work style — and what personal dream or project are you pouring energy into?

389. If you're a Springsteen fan, what's your anthem — and if not, why doesn't his music click for you?

390. What would you name your pirate ship to show your spirit — brave, wild, or magical?

391. What subject you studied in school has stuck with you and helped you most in your real life?

392. Other than money, what would you wish could grow on trees to bring more joy or ease into life?

393. Where would getting a boil be the most inconvenient or embarrassing?

394. What odd or surprising phobia have you heard about that made you do a double-take?

395. What inspiring or rocking new song title might Buddy Holly have created if he'd lived longer?

396. What lesson your parents drilled into you ended up being some of the best advice you've ever gotten?

397. If you could pick one candy to have unlimited forever, what sweet would you never get tired of?

398. What unexpected disaster would make brushing your teeth into a full-blown emergency?

399. What new skill or professional title would you love to have magically added to your resume?

400. Have you ever dreamed of being older — for freedom, respect, or new adventures?

401. Which color would make you hesitate before buying even your dream car?

402. If you could invent a clean, magical energy source, what would you call it to inspire the world?

403. What's something small or silly that tugged at your heart recently and made you cry?

404. If you woke up after 100 years, what changes in technology, culture, or people would surprise you most?

405. When you flipped a coin to decide something, what were the two things you were choosing between?

406. Have you ever hit the halfway mark in a book and decided to just let it go?

407. Which popular movie would you love to retitle for fun — and what would you call it?

408. If you disappeared into a bookstore, what section would your friends know to search for you?

409. What's the cringiest or least helpful thing someone could say when you're dealing with a breakup?

410. Which animal's power, size, or stealth do you think makes it the most deadly?

411. If you could dream up your own magical theme park, what would the theme be and what fun rides would it have?

412. If a cartoon character started a rap career, who would steal the spotlight and why?

413. How do you imagine our planet evolving over the next 10,000 years — more magical, more wild, or more wise?

414. Who's someone or what situation makes it hard for you to feel real sympathy, even when you want to?

415. Have you ever done a "pretend clean" by hiding everything messy in a closet before guests came over?

416. What made you last feel strong, bold, and ready to shout, "Bring it on!" to whatever came your way?

417. If you wanted to hide a funny message on the bottom of a boat for someone to find, what would it be?

418. If you designed a Monopoly game based on something you love, what would the theme and pieces be?

419. Have you ever bought something that seemed amazing, but later you thought, "Why did I spend my money on this?"

420. What drive-thru service idea would you find hilariously wrong or totally impractical?

421. If you could stuff a cart with your dream foods and drinks for free, what would you grab?

422. Have you ever used something odd — a receipt, a leaf, a candy wrapper — as a bookmark?

423. When was the last time you made a selfish choice — and how did it feel afterward?

424. Have you ever laughed at how someone's name matched exactly the job they ended up doing?

425. What gum brand do you reach for when you want something sweet, fresh, or comforting?

426. What type of salad dressing would match your spirit — something sweet, tangy, bold, or calm?

427. What's the last time something caught you by surprise and made you laugh for real?

428. What special piece of jewelry do you wear every day — and why does it matter to you?

429. What's a "BOGO" deal that would be pointless or funny for you — something you'd never need two of?

430. On a scale of pure pride to pure cringe, how embarrassing is your passport photo?

431. What odd museum display caught your attention and left you wondering, "Why is this here?"

432. If you were all alone, how much more freely would you dance — would you spin, jump, or just go wild?

433. If you could have a cat in any color, would you match it to your house or choose your favorite bright color?

434. If you flushed at someone else's place and it didn't work, what quick-thinking plan would you try?

435. Have you ever made toasty marshmallows by a fire — and when was the last time you had that sweet moment?

436. What mascot would you invent to show the heart and spirit of your hometown during the Olympics?

437. What color combo would make you secretly cry if a makeover show redid your bedroom?

438. If you could go back in time, which decade would you want your teenage years to happen in?

439. If you could pick your Power Ranger color, what color would make you feel strongest and happiest?

440. Can you rattle off a list of European capital cities — and which ones always come to your mind first?

441. Which pop diva would you love (or laugh) to see trying to lead a screaming heavy metal group?

442. If you could take a class in something creative, powerful, or just fun, what would it be?

443. If you could pick a fragrance that captured your energy and heart, what scent would it be?

444. What's one silly or embarrassing thing you did as a teenager that you now laugh (or blush) about?

445. If you could invent a colorful, magical board game, what unique pieces would players use?

446. What three songs have lived on your playlists through every phase of life?

447. What fun, silly, or useful ways could you use a ping-pong ball other than for table tennis?

448. If you reimagined Charlie's Angels with an all-male cast, which actors would make it awesome or hilarious?

449. What do you think turns everyday existence into vibrant, meaningful living?

450. Have you ever experienced déjà vu — that eerie feeling you were repeating a moment exactly?

451. If you started a bowling team with your friends, what fun or sassy team name would you choose?

452. If cobwebs came in bright or magical colors, would you find them charming or still clean them?

453. What's the oldest and most powerful natural thing you've encountered — and how did it make you feel?

454. When did you last mask your true feelings with a brave face — and how did you get through it?

455. When did you last experience truly thoughtful customer service while shopping — and what did you pick up?

456. If you could sit front row all season for any sports team, which one would you choose?

457. What board game brings you the most joy — cozy nights, laughter, or friendly competition?

458. When you make resolutions for the New Year, do you usually follow through — or give yourself grace when they change?

459. Would you be curious or scared about the idea of being frozen and waking up in the distant future?

460. How many B-named people — Brittanys, Brians, Bellas — are part of your life story?

461. What amazing deal did you once snag that still makes you smile or brag?

462. If cockroaches could chat, what hilarious or annoying things would they tell us about our messy kitchens?

463. When and where did you spot a parking job so bad it made you stop and take a photo?

464. If you could only have one kind of bread always, what delicious kind would you choose?

465. What's the simplest way you've ever earned money — a favor, a prize, an easy job?

466. Who deserves a surprise shout-out from you — for support, kindness, or just for being awesome?

467. What's the oddest or most surprising room you've wandered into — and what story do you tell about it?

468. How important do you think it is for animals to have strong legal protections like humans?

469. If Dorothy from Oz stepped into 2025, what stylish or surprising shoes would carry her down the Yellow Brick Road?

470. What's the last thing that sparked real wonder, amazement, or admiration in you?

471. If you could journey to any planet, where would you go to explore beauty, mystery, or adventure?

472. What quirky or unexpected item do you keep tucked away in your car's trunk "just in case"?

473. Did you ever enter a silly burping contest — and what happened when you tried?

474. What amazing optical illusion made you do a double take and question your eyes?

475. If dinosaurs came back, where would be the best place for them to live without causing trouble?

476. If someone started singing "Frère Jacques," would you join in confidently or just mumble along?

477. Which quiz category — no matter how hard you try — always seems to trip you up a little?

478. How do you recover gracefully or humorously after a high-five fail?

479. What's a time you doubted someone's crazy story, only to realize

480. If black holes came in friendly, beautiful colors, what shade would you imagine them to be?

481. When you think about it, how many gadgets at home are always beeping for your time or energy?

482. What's one way you know you could be less wasteful in your daily life, but haven't fixed yet?

483. If your week was a dance, what style — graceful ballet, fast salsa, or silly freestyle — would it be?

484. What app keeps you organized, and what silly app do you keep just because it makes you smile?

485. If you set out to rule the world, what surprising or strategic first move would you make?

486. If there was a superhero with a power that didn't really help anyone, what silly skill would it be?

487. What creative new fastener could replace Velcro — colorful, strong, or just fun?

488. What's your top ABBA song — and when it comes on, do you belt out every lyric without hesitation?

489. When was the last time you played with your food by making words with alphabet pasta?

490. If you could experience something amazing with nine people, what would it be and who would you bring?

491. What special features would turn your treehouse into the dream hideaway you've always wanted?

492. When did you last stand in a crazy long line — and what made you decide it was worth it?

493. When was the last time you pushed a door when you were supposed to pull — and how embarrassing was it?

494. What's the coolest or most helpful website you've stumbled onto that nobody else seems to know about?

495. What fun or daring hair color would you love to wear for just one day — neon, pastel, glittery?

496. Who do you know that's been married the longest — and what do you think is their secret?

497. If McDonald's made a cheeseburger-scented candle, would you light it for fun or avoid it completely?

498. If Elvis was living today, how would you picture him dressing — classic glam, trendy casual, or something totally different?

499. What's a moment when a child's honest, unexpected words completely caught you off guard?

500. Which vintage dance step — from the Twist to the Mashed Potato — do you love showing off (or laughing at)?

501. What's a silly or unforgettable super glue mishap you remember hearing about?

502. Have you experienced moments when a full moon made everything feel a little wilder or more magical?

503. What danger to humanity weighs most on your mind — and how do you stay hopeful about it?

504. If you knew someone who wanted to drive the Wienermobile, would you cheer them on — or laugh with them?

505. If you could drift off under the stars anywhere in the world, where would it be — a beach, desert, forest?

506. Have you ever been surprised by a food fight breaking out — and did you join in or run for cover?

507. What's the strangest, most "wait, what?!" moment you've witnessed in real life?

508. If you became a spy, what playful or mysterious code name would match your style?

509. What's the hottest thing you've seen outdoors — maybe a volcano, a fire, or desert sand?

510. What's a surprising or quirky fact you love to share to break the ice with people?

511. If you could rename the Monday morning blah feeling, what would your creative word be?

512. What color and special design would you choose to make your front door feel welcoming or stylish?

513. If everyone could magically know all the words to one song, what uplifting or meaningful song would you choose?

514. Have you ever gone out of your way to impress someone — and did it work or totally backfire?

515. What's a tattoo you saw that made you secretly wonder, "What were they thinking?"

516. Where were you the last time you truly exhaled and felt like everything was just right?

517. What's the one time you chose the laziest option — and it either worked out perfectly or hilariously failed?

518. If you got mistaken for a famous person by paparazzi, who would it be and what would you do next?

519. If the big red button was another color, what color would make you feel less curious about pushing it?

520. What fun or fancy title would you create to describe a boring household task and make it feel magical?

521. What's something you saw or heard lately that made you instantly sit up and pay attention?

522. How do you feel when you're alone — peaceful, creative, energized, or a little lonely?

523. What job out there do you think requires the most courage or carries the most danger?

524. What part of your body — your hands, your voice, your smile — would you insure like a celebrity might?

525. What's the oddest, quirkiest building you've entered — and what did you think of it?

526. If you could travel back in time to see a revolutionary invention presented, what would you choose?

527. What three things make you feel confident and proud because you're really good at them?

528. Would you rather drink from your pet's bowl or find another wild solution if you were really stuck?

529. What's one of the funniest things you've heard people saying without realizing you were listening?

530. When was the last time you gave your shoes a good polish — and did it feel like a lost art?

531. What's a colorful phrase you love that captures the feeling of trying again and again without giving up?

532. Where would your handwriting fall on a scale of 1 to 10 — and are you proud of it or shy about it?

533. What do you need for a workout to feel fulfilling — motivation, music, movement, or something else?

534. In your family, who can curl their tongue — and do you feel lucky (or left out) if you can or can't?

535. What's a cheesy country song title you've heard that made you giggle or roll your eyes?

536. Would you be curious or cautious about traveling in a driverless car — and why?

537. If you had to keep a suit of armor in your house, where would you put it to make it part of your style?

538. What Christmas cracker prize made you smile the most — a joke, a toy, or something totally random?

539. Where's the most surprising (or embarrassing) place you've ever drifted off for a nap?

540. Are you someone who follows the news each day — and what headline stood out for you today?

541. What's the funniest or cutest cat name you've ever come across?

542. What type of flooring would you love to have everywhere — cozy, stylish, or practical?

543. Have you ever been part of a campfire ghost story session — and what tale still gives you chills or giggles?

544. When was the last time you realized, "Maybe that wasn't the most sensitive thing to say"?

545. How would you quickly and simply explain how to brew the perfect cup of tea?

546. If one of your five senses could become incredibly powerful, which would you want it to be?

547. Have you ever heard of someone saving a fart in a jar as a joke — and did it make you laugh or cringe?

548. If you had a pencil in your hand right now, what would you find yourself drawing?

549. Have you ever come across a funny or unnecessary warning sign — and what did it say?

550. Can you think of a bunch of foods that start with "R" — and which one would you love to eat today?

551. When was your most recent moment of feeling totally bored — and how did you turn it around?

552. If you had to hide your squirrel snacks from sneaky thieves, where would you put them?

553. What delicious dip always wins your heart at parties or cozy nights in?

554. Do you believe letting athletes use special technology would make sports better — or less meaningful?

555. Which "just add water" item — food, toy, or handy tool — always makes you smile?

556. What's something about you that stands out as very different from how your parents live or think?

557. What fun, creative, or silly fitness trend would you love to introduce to the world?

558. Have you ever stubbornly kept clicking a dead remote — hoping maybe just one more press would fix it?

559. What's your favorite or most creative version of the classic "chicken crossing the road" joke?

560. Can you share a moment when you helped someone just because it felt right? What did you do?

561. Have you ever touched or held a strange or amazing animal? What animal was it?

562. Could you manage to get your socks on without using your hands if you absolutely had to?

563. Who is the most colorful or hilarious person you know — and what makes them such a character?

564. What's something silly, awkward, or unexpected that made you facepalm recently?

565. When was the last time you found yourself not knowing how to respond — and how did you handle it?

566. What's one small thing that always causes funny debates between you and your friends?

567. If you could have dinner with anyone from any time, who would be your dream dinner guest?

568. What's a funny or bizarre thing you think a news anchor would never say unless they totally lost it?

569. Do you know anyone who's done something crazy like microwaving their socks? Would you ever try it?

570. What's the silliest or most imaginative thing you could imagine filling a mattress with?

571. How many people in your life would you feel safe sharing a password with?

572. If you could invent a human experiment without worrying about right or wrong, what weird idea would you try?

573. If you knew the hidden trick to eternal youth, what would it be — simple, magical, or funny?

574. What old-school saying still pops out of your mouth, even if younger people laugh?

575. What quirky or surprising kind of yoga — with animals, laughter, or something else — would you love or avoid?

576. How would your day look if you suddenly had long, silly-looking index fingers?

577. What's one funny home video — yours or someone else's — that you could watch over and over?

578. If you had to choose between saving one child or two older adults, what would you decide — and why?

579. What's a time when someone said something shockingly sexist to you — and how did it make you feel?

580. When it comes to pumpkin pie, are you a full 10 fan or somewhere closer to a 2?

581. When was the last time you felt your heart race as you walked into a place — a meeting, party, or new adventure?

582. What famous band would you want playing to celebrate your life — joyful, emotional, or powerful music?

583. What three things — big or small — fill your heart with gratitude every time you think about them?

584. Have you ever jokingly answered the phone like a voicemail to make someone laugh?

585. At a candy counter, what treats always catch your eye before anything else?

586. If you were a book, would you be a bold adventure, a sweet romance, a thrilling mystery, or something totally unique?

587. What dreamy colors would you love to see soft, fluffy clouds painted in across the sky?

588. Did you love bouncing on the bed when you were a kid — and do you still wish you could sometimes?

589. What's the wildest or most unbelievable thing someone ever said to you — and did you believe them at first?

590. Which relative can you always count on to create those "Oh no!" moments during family gatherings?

591. If flavors disappeared but textures and colors remained, would you still explore different foods?

592. Have you ever had a quiet feeling or imagination about what your final chapter might look like?

593. Have you ever wandered through a maze and thought, "I might never get out of here"?

594. What's the most exciting thing you found when you were somewhere really dull or ordinary?

595. Have you ever jumped to the last page of a book because you couldn't wait to see what happens?

596. Which part of your usual routine feels the slowest or most tiresome?

597. If you were offered a parachute jump, would you feel excited, terrified, or a mix of both?

598. When was the last time you had to borrow money from a friend or family member — and how did it feel?

599. How would you gracefully survive being stuck beside someone with terrible BO on a bus or train?

600. How would you repurpose a single glove into something fun, useful, or surprising?

601. What cool or helpful ways could you use x-ray vision to make your life easier or more exciting?

602. What sound always makes you feel calm, cozy, or totally happy inside?

603. Have you ever finished a giant puzzle — and how many pieces did it have?

604. What's the most absurd "how did that happen?!" story you've heard about an accidental death?

605. Could getting rid of likes make social media healthier and help people care less about judgment?

606. Have you ever been in a place where you felt like you knew way more or could do much more than everyone else?

607. What's the worst, weirdest, or most hilarious gift you've ever been given?

608. When you celebrate Thanksgiving, what matters most — being together, giving thanks, or sharing special food?

609. What's a classic movie cliché that you realize hardly ever happens in everyday life?

610. If you could choose a dreamy or fun new color for all the grass in the world, what would you pick?

611. If you could only keep one kitchen appliance for cooking, what would it be — and why?

612. What's the cutest or silliest explanation about babies that made you laugh when you first heard it?

613. How many pink things can you list off the top of your head in just ten seconds?

614. How far have you ever jogged — and was it a race, an adventure, or just a surprising moment?

615. If you were brave enough to chase storms, what kind of wild weather would you pick to follow?

616. What was the last sweet, messy, or funny thing that made your fingers sticky?

617. Have you ever said yes to a blind date — and how did it turn out?

618. How do you emotionally respond when you see someone who is homeless — and does it inspire you to act?

619. If you could have a cozy home anywhere on Earth, what country would you choose?

620. What other surprising or useful ways have you used a simple handkerchief?

621. When did you last splash through a puddle — and did it feel silly, freeing, or just plain fun?

622. If you started a new cat food company, what cute or clever name would you come up with?

623. What's the biggest worry or concern quietly sitting in your heart at this moment?

624. Are marmalade sandwiches a yes, no, or maybe for you — and have you ever thought about trying one?

625. What's the craziest "As Seen on TV" invention that you actually considered buying (even for a second)?

626. When did you last pretend you didn't know something — and what happened next?

627. Are there things you prefer buying lots of instead of just picking the highest quality — and why?

628. If you suddenly floated into the air, what funny objects would you crash into before reaching the roof?

629. What three things are you looking forward to that make your heart feel lighter when you think about them?

630. If your initials created a silly virus name, what funny symptoms would it give people?

631. What hidden gem or hilarious object have you ever found tucked away in your couch?

632. If you could cannonball into a pool full of anything, what dream substance would it be?

633. What's a funny time when you spun yourself silly or ended up totally dizzy?

634. What's one piece of silly or strange trivia you know that makes people laugh or raise an eyebrow?

635. If you built your dream home, what special rooms would you add beyond the usual ones?

636. If crayons were edible, which one would you dare to nibble — based on the prettiest or yummiest-looking color?

637. Are there any classic songs or artists your parents loved that you now secretly (or proudly) enjoy too?

638. What's the most absurd or funny rule you've ever been asked to follow — even though you knew it was silly?

639. If Greyhound needed a new logo animal, what fun or powerful creature would you pick instead?

640. Which friend or family member just can't help spilling secrets (even if they don't mean to)?

641. What's a crime story you've heard where the criminal's mistake was so silly it made you laugh?

642. If you could put a life-sized animal sculpture in your house, what creature would you choose?

643. Which friend do you think would invent something really helpful — and what might it be for?

644. Where were you and what were you doing when the temperature felt absolutely unbearable?

645. If you had to pretend to be a regular person by day, what job would help you hide your superhero life?

646. When it comes to trifles, which layer could you happily eat by itself because it's so good?

647. Do you believe artists should tour less to help the environment — or find greener ways to perform?

648. If someone was oddly afraid of hot dogs, what funny name would you give to their "phobia"?

649. When you were at the highest point on a Ferris wheel, what beautiful sights stretched out below you?

650. Which crime strikes you as the most heartbreaking or terrible to imagine happening?

651. If humans lived in zoos, what cozy, fun, or interesting things would you want in your habitat?

652. What outdoor adventure would you like to experience — even if it scares you a little?

653. Have you ever had a "Grinch moment" — and how did it happen?

654. If you could lead anything — a team, a mission, or a project — what would it be?

655. If breakfast could be dessert every day, what treat would you wake up excited for?

656. What was the last magical request you made to Santa Claus — whether you got it or not?

657. What's something you thought would be easy but realized was much harder once you started?

658. What's the biggest or funniest lie you've ever told — and what happened afterward?

659. If your kettle could talk, what sweet, funny, or sassy things would it say when it's working hard?

660. If you stumbled across $20 while staying in a hotel, what would you do — and why?

661. Have you given your car or any other objects a special or funny name? What are they?

662. What's the best waterslide memory you have — full of fun, fear, or laughter?

663. If you had to choose between saving a person or an animal, what would you do — and how would it affect you?

664. If you could make a silly or clever moon landing quote, what would you yell stepping onto the surface?

665. What's a surefire way to say the wrong thing and wreck a first date — even if it's hilariously bad?

666. As silly as it sounds, have you ever tried to burp the whole alphabet — and what letter did you reach?

667. What qualities make a pop song so good that you can't help but sing along every time?

668. How much do you let other people's opinions shape your feelings — and how do you protect your self-confidence?

669. What's a funny or bizarre breakup reason you've heard — the kind that made you laugh instead of cry?

670. Would you take the daring leap across rooftops if it meant survival, even if fear screamed "no"?

671. Which accent feels warm, stylish, or lovely to you when someone speaks it?

672. If you could invent a sweet or clever new utensil by combining two others, what would it be called?

673. When was the last time you made tea for someone special — and how did it feel to share that moment?

674. If you invented a colorful, delicious new veggie, what would its name be and how would it taste?

675. Living in a lighthouse sounds dreamy — but what lonely or challenging part would be hardest for you?

676. What creative way would you imagine faking your death — and where would you secretly go afterward?

677. What's the funniest emergency room visit story you've heard — something wild and unexpected?

678. Whose beautiful or super tidy handwriting do you wish you had in your family or friends circle?

679. As a kid (or maybe even now), did you ever wonder about — and test — whether the fridge light turns off?

680. If you created a gym with a unique twist, what fun or empowering name would you call it?

681. Do you keep any old, cozy socks around because they feel too comfy (or sentimental) to toss?

682. What word becomes funny, strange, or just weird when you repeat it a bunch of times out loud?

683. Have you ever made a goofy attempt to lick your elbow — and did it end with laughs?

684. What's the most unusual or "only a celebrity would do this" baby name you've come across?

685. Which delicious cuisine would you love to learn from a professional chef in a private class?

686. If Winnie-the-Pooh got a fashion upgrade, what adorable or stylish outfit would you pick for him?

687. When you were last feeling sick, what made you feel the worst — and what helped you feel better?

688. If your friends scored you on dependability, what would they say makes you trustworthy (or not)?

689. What's a crossword clue you figured out that made you feel like a genius for a moment?

690. If your outdoor picnic got rained on, how would you turn the day into a fun and cozy memory anyway?

691. If you had to make music with what's around you, what three items would you grab first?

692. If you were a mischievous supervillain, what clever or wicked name would you give yourself?

693. In your heart, do you feel like good people still outnumber the bad — and what gives you that hope?

694. What travel mishap turned into an unforgettable (and maybe hilarious) adventure?

695. Have you ever taken on the fun (or silly) challenge of running up a down escalator?

696. What's the craziest, funniest, or most amazing ride you've seen while on the road?

697. Have you ever played leapfrog — and if you tried it today, would you still land on your feet?

698. If you had to pick just one thing to stockpile for a long stay at home, what would it be?

699. What things do you do automatically, almost like you're on autopilot, without thinking about it?

700. Which friend or family member becomes surprisingly fierce or scary when they get mad?

701. When was the last time you stayed in bed all day just for relaxation — not because you were sick?

702. What's something you once thought was true or helpful, but had to relearn differently?

703. If you drew your life so far as a line, would it zigzag, spiral, climb, dip — or something else?

704. Which Starburst flavor do you love most — and would you pick a whole bag of just that one?

705. When you talk about your dreams or promises, how often do you turn them into reality?

706. What's the funniest or most unbelievable catwalk outfit you've ever seen or heard about?

707. When did you last jump rope, and do any of those childhood songs or chants still stick with you?

708. What would be a softer, funnier, or more colorful thing to wave for surrender instead of a white flag?

709. What's the loudest machine or gadget in your house — and do you secretly love or hate the noise?

710. If you could have a thoughtful afternoon tea with any leader in history, who would you invite?

711. What song do you secretly wish you could ban forever because you've heard it too many times?

712. When you were little, did you play the "cooties" game — and who was usually the "cootie carrier"?

713. What's a meal or snack you remember that made you feel super thirsty?

714. When you dream about your future, do you imagine feeling even more joyful than today?

715. Out of all the email addresses you have, which one feels most "you" — and why?

716. What small but creative "punishment" would you invent for people who abandon their carts in parking lots?

717. Have you ever made a funny or serious attempt to sneeze with your eyes wide open?

718. Is there a retro device or old-school tech item you refuse to upgrade because it still makes you happy?

719. What favorite childhood pajamas made you feel cozy, happy, or just totally cool?

720. If you had to imagine your nose as a piece of fruit, what colorful or cute fruit would it be?

721. When's the most desperate time you had to hold it in — and how did you survive the adventure?

722. Have you ever gone way underground — to a subway, a cave, or another secret place? How was it?

723. If you created a brand-new search engine, what creative or catchy name would you dream up?

724. What shoes in your life brought you the most joy — comfortable, stylish, or unforgettable?

725. When does chilly turn into "nope, I'm staying in with a blanket" for you?

726. If you could snap your fingers and speak a new language, which one would open exciting doors for you?

727. In a parallel world, what would you swap into the middle — a unicorn, a spaceship, or something totally random?

728. Have you ever had a travel moment that turned into a travel mess — but now makes you laugh?

729. When reading, do you find yourself catching other people's errors faster than noticing your own?

730. Is there a beautiful culture that you love learning about, but think would be hard to live in for real?

731. Who among your family or friends feels like the living definition of kindness and honesty?

732. Have you ever given a quick hair trim to a friend — or would you if they begged you for help?

733. If you could wear animal ears for a day, whose would you choose — maybe floppy bunny ears or sleek cat ears?

734. Which catchy mnemonic do you still remember — and how did it save you in school (or life)?

735. What loving or unique names do you call your grandparents — and do they have a story behind them?

736. What sweet, crunchy, or colorful toppings make a frozen yogurt absolutely perfect for you?

737. If you were a delicious three-course meal, what would be your starter, main dish, and sweet dessert?

738. What are three things you own that you wouldn't miss right away if they vanished?

739. Have you ever had a moment when a slip-up or "bad" choice ended up opening a good new path?

740. Should the world completely ban fossil fuels — and what changes would you hope to see instead?

741. If you could perform one dazzling magic trick, what would it be — and who would you wow with it?

742. Do you think you're the most competitive among your friends — or is someone else even more intense?

743. Where's the most random or funny place you discovered your missing remote?

744. What double-dare challenge did you take on that you still laugh (or cringe) about today?

745. Do you believe future generations could live in a world without hunger — and what would it take?

746. What's the funniest or most amazing thing you've seen someone carry on their head?

747. If the only thing you could grab right now had to protect you from zombies, how would you do?

748. If you could invent a dreamy new spread from your favorite food, what would it be?

749. Have you ever taken a leap into a giant pile of autumn leaves — and do you miss doing it?

750. If you got to design a crop circle prank, what funny shape or picture would you make?

751. Was there a game you couldn't stop playing — and looking back, do you still smile thinking about it?

752. What film from the last year made you laugh (or groan) because it was just so badly made?

753. Do you still hold onto any old CDs — and what was the last one you couldn't resist buying?

754. What's one of the saddest or scariest stories of medical mistakes you've come across?

755. What stylish or bold designer sunglasses would you love to own?

756. If you could make it "rain" anything fun or surprising, what would fall from the sky?

757. Have you ever acted like you understood something just to avoid feeling awkward? What was it?

758. What fun accessories — hats, scarves, buttons — do you think make a snowman truly special?

759. Would you brave three crocodiles to grab a million dollars — or come up with a clever plan instead?

760. What random, forgotten thing did you once find tucked away in your pocket?

761. Who among your family or friends would rock a belly dancing outfit and moves the best?

762. Do you think Bigfoot could really be out there, hiding somewhere — or is it just a myth?

763. What's something you were too hard on yourself for lately — and how could you show yourself more grace?

764. If you had to pick a warm, cozy place to "fly south" to for winter, where would it be?

765. What's your favorite day of the year (other than your birthday) — and why does it mean so much to you?

766. What heartfelt or inspiring words would you love to say as your final message?

767. What playful or wild word would you make up to describe a number that's bigger than you can count?

768. What's the wisest or most moving thing you've ever been told — something that still resonates today?

769. If you crafted your dream mocktail, what tasty flavors would you mix — and what catchy name would you give it?

770. What's a time when your frustration got the best of you and you threw something silly or dramatic?

771. Do you believe we'll one day find out who Banksy really is — or is the mystery part of the magic?

772. Have you ever seen a product where you thought, "Did anyone even need this?" but it still caught on?

773. If lies caused flaming pants, would you be safe today — or running for a fire extinguisher?

774. When was the last time you felt so joyful or rebellious that you wanted to throw caution to the wind?

775. When did you last pedal away on a bike — and where did you go?

776. What sweet or playful new name would you invent for a Hershey's Kiss?

777. If you went through astronaut training, what skill would you master the fastest?

778. If you had to give a talk tomorrow, what personal passion or interest would you share with others?

779. Which YouTuber do you love watching — someone who makes you laugh, think, or learn something new?

780. How wonderfully quirky are you on a 1 to 10 scale — and what makes you delightfully different?

781. What's the sound word (like splash, zip, or boom) that always makes you smile?

782. If you could pick a fun or fierce cowboy/cowgirl name, what would it be?

783. When did you last dance in a big, silly conga line — and how did it make you feel?

784. If you could get anything you want delivered instantly, what would it be — a treat, a gift, or something fun?

785. If you stumbled across a mysterious plant, what colors, shapes, or smells would it have — and what would you call it?

786. What moment or feeling do you think captures the true meaning of bliss?

787. If your friends entered a plate-spinning contest, who would surprise everyone and win?

788. What are three privileges or freedoms that kids often dream about having when they grow up?

789. What fun or magical sound would you love to hear instead of Big Ben's serious "bong" every hour?

790. If you were a Transformer, what fabulous or fun vehicle would show off your personality best?

791. What healthy habits help you release your emotions and regain your calm?

792. How many emotions do you think you could show without saying a single word?

793. What's one trend that everyone seems to love but leaves you scratching your head?

794. How long could you keep a plank before your muscles screamed "enough"?

795. What time in history would you love to visit — just for a day — to see life in a different world?

796. If you had to let go of a friend at work, how would you stay kind while still doing what's needed?

797. How do you calm down a bad cramp — any tricks you swear by?

798. Did you ever trip over your shoelaces — and was it a graceful fall or a total wipeout?

799. What's a voicemail message you heard that made you smile, laugh, or feel totally welcomed?

800. Are there any small habits or behaviors you repeat often, even when you don't need to?

801. If the internet ever broke for real, what do you think would be the biggest reason?

802. What home fitness item would you want most — something that motivates you and fits your style?

803. Has there been someone you once saw as larger-than-life — and do you still feel the same today?

804. If you had to give your country a fun shape name — like Italy's "boot" — what would you pick?

805. Have you ever been on a diet that sounded great but felt miserable — and what happened?

806. When your braces were removed, how did you mark the big day — smiles, parties, or treats?

807. What sweet, crunchy, or fruity topping would make Shredded Wheat perfect for you?

808. Imagine your pet wrote you a job reference — would it be glowing with praise or full of funny truths?

809. What thoughtful or funny secret Santa gift did you last give — and how did it turn out?

810. Have you ever joined in and twerked — whether it was at a party, a dance class, or just for a laugh?

811. If you tunneled to the center of the Earth, what surprising or magical thing do you think you might find?

812. Do you think our generation can end single-use plastics — and what hopeful steps are you seeing?

813. What's the craziest or wobbliest thing you've ever balanced on when you couldn't reach something?

814. If "Death by Chocolate" exists, what sweet or spicy food do you think deserves a warning too?

815. When has your stomach betrayed you with loud noises at the most embarrassing moment?

816. Is saying "blonde moment" fair or harmful — and why might it need to change?

817. Have you ever seen a place name so funny you had to laugh — where was it?

818. When did you last hear birdsong — and did it bring you a sense of calm, joy, or nostalgia?

819. If you designed a lovely new carpet shampoo, what fresh scent would it have and what would you name it?

820. What's the best or funniest word you've ever played in Scrabble — and did it win you the game?

821. Which friend or family member is the buffet queen or king, always finding room for one more plate?

822. What's the ouchiest thing you've ever stepped on barefoot — and how long did you hop around?

823. How often do you find yourself wishing more people used good old-fashioned common sense?

824. Which current world event would you find hardest to break down in a gentle way for a child?

825. If James Bond had to choose a new drink, what funny or unexpected choice would totally change his image?

826. Which friend would you pick to tie up to and race with — someone with great teamwork or great laughs?

827. Have you ever blurted out something you were thinking without meaning to? How did people react?

828. What's a silly or polite way you've heard people say they're going to the bathroom?

829. What would you do to stay calm and kind if you're stuck next to a crying baby for hours on a plane?

830. Do you believe in the idea that the kindness (or meanness) we give comes back to us someday?

831. What's the funniest or most heartwarming thing that's happened to you during a team training event?

832. If you could be a tree, would you rather stand tall and proud or be short and strong?

833. If you could name a beautiful new galaxy, what magical or inspiring name would you choose?

834. If you could magically have one room or part of your home professionally redone, what would it be?

835. If you could take a meaningful pilgrimage, where would you go and why would it matter to you?

836. Do you believe humans might achieve eternal life someday through science — and would you want that?

837. Can you make cool beatboxing sounds, or would your best effort be more funny than fancy?

838. If you think about Scotland, what are three things — sounds, sights, or traditions — you picture first?

839. Would you support famous sports players quitting social media to avoid racial abuse and protect their well-being?

840. If you could magically have bright-colored skin, what fun color would you pick for yourself?

841. Have you heard of any truly miraculous escape stories that amazed or inspired you?

842. What was the last library visit you had like — did you check out a good book or just explore?

843. Are there extreme cases where you believe stealing could be morally acceptable?

844. Would you take the risk and visit a real-life Jurassic Park if you had the chance?

845. What's a story you've heard about someone getting revenge in a way that was clever but not cruel?

846. Can you remember a time when you felt someone's eyes on you — and how did it make you feel?

847. Who would be in your personal team of seven heroes, adventurers, or close friends?

848. Which celebrities or inspiring people were also born on the same day as you?

849. Have you ever heard a hilarious or unbelievable car insurance story that made you shake your head?

850. Will there still be shopping malls and stores in the future — or will everything move online?

851. Which actor-turned-singer made you think, "Maybe music wasn't the best idea"?

852. Should students ever be expelled from school — and when, if ever, do you think it's right?

853. How do you stay organized with appointments and deadlines — and what tool or method helps you most?

854. Can you recall a time when letting go of your pride helped you handle a tough situation?

855. What terrifying experience — whether you lived it or watched it — still sticks in your memory?

856. Have you ever tucked something away so well for safekeeping that you couldn't find it later?

857. What inspiring or adventurous ending would you imagine for yourself — something bold and unforgettable?

858. If laughter comes first, what's second-best for making you feel better — music, hugs, nature?

859. What's your ultimate milkshake flavor — sweet, nostalgic, or a little adventurous?

860. Would you consider joining a clinical study for money — and what's the minimum you'd expect?

861. Have you ever sent a hilarious autocorrect mistake that made people laugh (or gasp)?

862. What tiny body part (like a pinky toe or earlobe) could you live without if you had to?

863. Have you ever believed in a lucky charm — maybe a piece of jewelry, a keepsake, or a small treasure?

864. What fun or silly thing have you bought recently just because it made you happy?

865. Have you ever been caught under a bird (or other animal) when it decided to "go"? What happened?

866. Which three online stores do you find yourself clicking on most when shopping for clothes, gifts, or home stuff?

867. Which friend would you be nervous about leaving your house or pets with — and why?

868. Can you remember a moment when someone's words stung deeply — and how you healed from it?

869. If you blended three of your favorite candy bars into one, what fun name would you invent?

870. What's something you refuse to believe — even if the whole world says otherwise?

871. Did you discover any books through school reading lists that you ended up loving?

872. If you had to pick someone alive today who should never be President, who would it be?

873. Have you ever experienced a moment when you felt unseen or misinterpreted by others?

874. What's the weirdest or most unforgettable story you've heard of someone swallowing something unusual?

875. What color would you choose for Little Red Riding Hood's cloak if it weren't red — and how would it change her story?

876. What's the most charming or sophisticated garden decoration you've admired?

877. Which recipe book is your most trusted kitchen companion — the one with the pages full of stains and love?

878. If you created a signature perfume or cologne, what beautiful or playful name would you call it?

879. What's a time when you made a spontaneous decision that turned into a beautiful memory?

880. If you could make up a fun nickname for the skin on your nose, what would it be?

881. What makes us human in your eyes — is it love, curiosity, compassion, or something else?

882. What single thing about your future would you be most curious to find out?

883. Have you ever gotten completely covered in mud — and what were you doing?

884. Have you ever seen a really funny or strange Top 5 list that made you laugh or shake your head?

885. What warm or comforting cooked foods would you miss the most if you had to eat only raw foods?

886. If you could plan a dream New Year's celebration with your friends, where would you choose?

887. Have you ever seen a restaurant with a name that was super clever or funny? What was it?

888. Do you think humans are the most advanced, or are there more amazing creatures yet to be discovered?

889. Have you ever felt that doing what was "right" made a situation harder or more complicated?

890. What moment of pain — physical or emotional — stands out most in your memory, and how would you score it?

891. Have you ever come across an invention that seemed totally silly or unnecessary? What was it?

892. When did you last come up with a clever fix at the very last minute to save the day?

893. If your surname had to be a fun or fancy food name, what would you pick?

894. What three behaviors or choices would you find hardest to forgive in someone else?

895. Would you trim someone else's toenails if they needed help — like an elderly loved one?

896. Can you remember a time when you heard someone say something so snobby it stuck with you?

897. What color would you pick for a tooth implant if it could be something playful instead of plain white?

898. What's something you rarely shop for that most people seem to buy all the time?

899. What memory, if any, from this week do you think you'll still be talking about next year?

900. What's your best memory of turning an ordinary at-home week into a great adventure?

901. Has anyone guessed your age totally wrong — and how did it make you feel?

902. Have you ever given a really generous tip after receiving truly wonderful service? What happened?

903. If your online usernames became a band name, which one would be the catchiest or most fun?

904. What's the most fun or amazing experiment you've ever done — like making slime, a volcano, or crystals?

905. Are you someone who would offer someone a third chance — or does trust have limits for you?

906. What's a time when you said something or expected a reaction — and were met with pure silence?

907. If you were a travel destination, what place would reflect your energy — peaceful beach, vibrant city, or cozy village?

908. Is there a celebrity home you've seen that made you think, "Wow, that's really bad taste"?

909. If you could go behind the scenes at any big event, where would you love to have VIP passes?

910. What's the most towering place you've visited where you stood and looked out over everything?

911. Who inspires you by living boldly and making the most out of every single day?

912. What unique or comforting potato dish would you invent for a fun dinner with friends or family?

913. Do you believe in spirits or ghosts — and have you ever had a moment that made you wonder?

914. What's the funniest or most creative shower curtain you've ever seen in someone's house or a store?

915. Do you think it's right or wrong for art galleries and museums to take money from fossil-fuel businesses?

916. Have you ever had the luxury of flying first class — and if you could choose, what airline would you fly with?

917. Have you ever seen something so strange for sale that you couldn't believe it was real?

918. If you could design a brand-new app for fun, wellness, or creativity, what would it be like?

919. Is there a true crime story that really stuck with you — something shocking or heartbreaking?

920. What's the longest you've let dirty dishes stack up before you decided to clean them?

921. What's one behavior you find extremely rude or disrespectful?

922. Were you ever bullied as a child — and how did that experience shape you?

923. Have you ever gone along with something awkward or cringey just to be polite? What happened?

924. Do you believe someone can truly appreciate joy if they've never experienced sadness?

925. If you were a rapper, what creative or fierce name would you want to go by?

926. What's one part of your life where it's hardest for you to stick to your goals?

927. Have you ever read about a shocking experiment that made you think, "That would never happen now"?

928. Have you ever gotten seasick on a boat trip or cruise? What helped you feel better?

929. What's the most random thing you've tossed into your shopping cart just because it made you smile?

930. Do you hit your fitness goals for weekly exercise, or are you still working on it?

931. Have you ever seen a magic trick that left you completely stunned and wondering how it was done?

932. If you could film any amazing wildlife moment, what would you hope to see through your camera?

933. What spooky sound have you heard that gave you chills — even if you didn't know what it was?

934. Have you ever swum in a river — and was it fun, refreshing, or a little bit scary?

935. Have you ever been asked something super personal or rude that totally caught you off guard?

936. What was the last surprising sight or moment that made you stop and look again?

937. What's the coolest or weirdest thing you know about the human body that you love to share?

938. Were hand-me-downs part of your childhood — and would you still love a good secondhand find today?

939. Have you ever seen a paint name so strange or funny that it made you laugh?

940. Who is the most graceful, polished, and elegant person you know?

941. Have you ever received a compliment that was so odd it left you wondering if it was really a compliment?

942. Have you ever felt embarrassed after calling someone by the wrong name for way too long?

943. Can you remember a time when you skipped showers for days — and why?

944. Which famous women do you think have the most beautiful or powerful sense of style?

945. What adventurous, wild, or bold thing have you ever done — and would you do it again?

946. Do you still enjoy listening to the songs you loved ten years ago, or has your playlist changed a lot?

947. If you saw someone badly hurt and bleeding, would you know what to do? Have you ever had to help?

948. Should scary movies still be made today, or are they no longer helpful or needed?

949. What small personality trait would you let go of if you could — something you find a little annoying about yourself?

950. If you hibernated all winter, what delicious food would you be most excited to eat first?

951. Have you put together anything from a kit lately — and did you enjoy the process?

952. What is something that costs money today that you wish was free for everyone?

953. Have you ever had to find your way using a traditional map — and did it go smoothly or not?

954. Is there anyone in your family whose name you're really glad you didn't end up with?

955. Have you ever read about a strange or gross old-time remedy people used to believe in?

956. If you didn't have enough plates at a party, what fun or funny alternative would you use?

957. What science project disaster from school still makes you laugh or cringe today?

958. What extra limb would you add to your body if you had to — and what would you use it for?

959. What silly or sweet names would you invent for the family of bears in Goldilocks?

960. Do you believe that too many choices can sometimes make life more stressful instead of more free?

961. What little rituals or treats make you realize the weekend is really here?

962. Do you sometimes feel younger or older than your actual age deep down inside?

963. Have you ever heard of a hoarding story that really shocked or saddened you?

964. If veggie bacon needed a new name that sounded yummy, what creative idea would you suggest?

965. What's the most recent thing you needed to swap batteries for — and was it easy or annoying?

966. Have you ever been tempted by an infomercial product — and did you actually buy it?

967. Have you ever spotted a product with a name so funny it made you laugh out loud?

968. Have you started playing any board games online now instead of around the table?

969. What kind of moments — sweet, sad, or powerful — tend to make you tear up?

970. What sweet and catchy name would you invent to replace "Toot Sweets" if you had the chance?

971. Have you ever had to pay a huge, unexpected repair bill — and what broke?

972. When did you last peek through your fingers while watching something you couldn't quite handle?

973. What's something special you do to make your home welcoming when visitors are coming?

974. Do you add "shoot" when playing "rock, paper, scissors," or do you just go straight to the move?

975. When was the last time you felt totally lost — and how did you find your way back?

976. What unusual, magical, or wild place would you love to have a party in?

977. What's the most fun or unexpected moment you had during a school field day?

978. Have you ever gone for a swim without a bathing suit — where and when did it happen?

979. Have you ever gotten a fortune cookie message that felt perfect or special at just the right time?

980. Who inspires you with their real-life acts of bravery or kindness?

981. Which friend's laugh always makes you smile because it's just so unique or silly?

982. What music has been filling your space today — anything calming, energetic, or emotional?

983. What creative or silly dog-breed mix would you invent with a name like "goldendoodle" or "cockapoo"?

984. What clever or funny riddle do you like to tell to stump people (or make them laugh)?

985. If you had to have a scar, where would you want it — somewhere hidden or somewhere you'd show proudly?

986. What's a movie that made you roll your eyes at the plot — but you still loved it for the fun of it?

987. What three sports would you mix together to create a brand-new, exciting sport?

988. What's something you look back on and think, "Wow, that was a huge waste of my time"?

989. When have you found yourself saying, "Life is like a box of chocolates" — and did it fit the moment?

990. If you had to make up a word that captured the sound of cheese melting, what would it sound like?

991. If you could name a new element, what would you call it — something magical, scientific, or personal?

992. What would you love to swipe away forever with a dab of magical disappearing cream?

993. What's something that brought a spark of excitement to your life this year?

994. Which food spot would you love to get free meals from forever — your dream food heaven?

995. Where have you been that felt magical, unexplored, or like a true adventure into the unknown?

996. What would be a terrible, hilarious, or gross sandwich filling you definitely wouldn't want to try?

997. Do you think it can ever be acceptable to take matters into your own hands instead of following the law?

998. What do you believe happens when two impossible forces meet — and how would you explain it?

999. If snakes had fluffy fur instead of sleek skin, would you like them more, less, or about the same?

1000. If a Star Wars movie had a totally silly line, what would you imagine it to be?

1001. If you had a world quiz, how many cities that start with "B" could you name without help?

1002. If you realize a cashier overpaid you in change, what would you do?

1003. If you had to hide 101 adorable dalmatians from sight, where would you put them?

1004. If you had to rename Harry Potter with something totally funny or silly, what would you pick?

1005. Have you ever given away a gift you received because you thought someone else would like it more?

1006. If you could fill your retirement with joyful hobbies, what would you choose to do most?

1007. If someone dislikes haters, are they just another hater, or are they standing up for kindness?

1008. Which movie had an explosion so amazing it made you want to watch it again and again?

1009. Can you think of someone who thinks they're brilliant but often misses the mark?

1010. What was the last thoughtful or fun gift you picked for someone's birthday?

1011. Can you remember a time when too many choices made a decision stressful instead of fun?

1012. If your emotions were a picture today, what kind of image would it be?

1013. At what point did you have your longest hair — and was it a style choice or a phase?

1014. What are the little signs — habits, moods, actions — that show you're feeling stressed?

1015. Do you answer calls from unknown numbers, or do you prefer to let them ring through?

1016. What would you do if someone next to you at dinner made really loud eating noises — say something or stay quiet?

1017. If you had a huge cardboard cutout of The Rock, where would you tuck it away in your home?

1018. Are there any sounds that instantly make you wince or feel irritated?

1019. When was the last time you had hiccups — and what strange or funny thing did you do to get rid of them?

1020. Which Monopoly token feels lucky or special to you — and why do you like it?

1021. When did you last empathize deeply by imagining what life is like for someone very different from you?

1022. Have you recently changed your mind at the last minute — about an event, purchase, or plan?

1023. If you had to pretend that a super unhealthy food was healthy, how would you advertise it?

1024. Is there a sweet or silly nursery rhyme you can still recite without missing a beat?

1025. Are you someone who struggles to let go of grudges — and if so, is one still lingering in your heart?

1026. What's your most unforgettable moment in a public changing room — funny, sweet, or awkward?

1027. If you could hypnotize someone in your family, what funny or sweet thing would you have them do?

1028. Is there a cute nickname that you really don't enjoy being called by others?

1029. Have you ever agreed to something you didn't want to do just because someone convinced you?

1030. What three qualities make someone a lifelong friend to you?

1031. Which canned fruit do you secretly think tastes better than the fresh one?

1032. What's the guitar riff that instantly makes you smile or sing along?

1033. How many single-use items sneak into your life each week — and is it something you notice?

1034. What silly or punny dad joke never fails to make you laugh or roll your eyes?

1035. Which famous chef's recipes sound like food disasters to your taste buds?

1036. What's a new skill you believe you could confidently learn in just a month?

1037. If Middle Earth existed today, what place would feel the most like it to you?

1038. If you meet someone who's clearly making things up but charming everyone else, how do you react?

1039. If you could rebrand guinea pigs, what cute or funny new name would you come up with?

1040. What's your go-to comfort food that always feels like a warm hug?

1041. When did you last enjoy walking barefoot outside — and what was the experience like?

1042. What was the fanciest or most costly meal you've ever treated yourself to?

1043. Who's the most artistic, whimsical, or creatively free person in your circle?

1044. What triggers your inner "worry mode," even if you know you're probably overthinking?

1045. What's your personal record for eating toast in one go — and do you remember why?

1046. What's your favorite kind of facial hair — classic, rugged, stylish, or quirky?

1047. What funny or clever ways did your parents use to help you survive chickenpox without scratching too much?

1048. What furry, feathery, or scaly friend did you wish for as a child but could never bring home?

1049. If money didn't exist, what would you love to receive in exchange for your work or help?

1050. What's a moment recently when you felt deep certainty about something important to you?

1051. Have you ever nicknamed someone "Fancy-Pants" because of a fabulous outfit they wore?

1052. What's the nastiest or most uncomfortable sound you've ever heard?

1053. Which chatterbox friend would you jokingly love to have a mute button for?

1054. If you could snap your fingers and become amazing at one martial art, which would you pick?

1055. What's a sweet, funny, or unforgettable thing you've seen while people-watching at an airport?

1056. When a spider shows up at home, are you brave, cautious, or do you call someone else to handle it?

1057. Is there something you eat that you've never seen how it looks growing or before it's prepared?

1058. How many clocks do you have ticking around your home — and do they all tell the same time?

1059. What special item would you love to bring home from another country — something meaningful or fun?

1060. Which dog breed feels like the best fit for your energy and personality?

1061. If you could make a soap with a totally unique scent, what would it smell like?

1062. What's the most creative or unusual way you've seen someone tie up their hair?

1063. Have you ever heard a conspiracy theory that made you wonder if it could be true?

1064. What age feels like the right time to you for welcoming children into your life?

1065. Do you believe you're artistic — and how do you express your creativity?

1066. What clever or crafty idea would you have for reusing an empty ice cream container?

1067. What delicious or homemade food would you share with royal guests at your house?

1068. In your heart, what global issue do you hope technology will help solve in the next few years?

1069. Do you have a journal where you write your thoughts — and how often do you use it?

1070. Have you ever heard a family name that made you giggle or do a double take?

1071. When did you last have that fluttery, excited feeling in your stomach before something important?

1072. When was the last time you said or did something that made you think, "I'm turning into my parents!"?

1073. What do you believe: Is it more fair to consider someone innocent until proven guilty?

1074. What shadow puppet do you love making when playing with a flashlight or campfire?

1075. Who was the most daring, unforgettable performer you've ever seen in concert or on stage?

1076. What's your must-have grilled food when it's barbecue season?

1077. If you had to turn curtains into a dress or outfit, which room's curtains would you grab first?

1078. What's the last thing you made completely from scratch — and was it a triumph or a learning moment?

1079. Would you ski jump for $1,000 — or would the fear be too great?

1080. What's the best basketball trick shot you've ever witnessed — something amazing or funny?

1081. Who's the friend who can pull off the funniest or scariest evil laugh?

1082. What's the funniest or most creative email address you've ever encountered?

1083. When was the last time you felt free enough to dance or sing outside in the rain?

1084. What land animal would be fascinating to see diving and swimming under the sea?

1085. If you were a WWE superstar, what strong or fierce (or silly) name would you pick?

1086. If you were a movie-style assassin, what "villain" or bad guy would you go after first (fictional only)?

1087. Do you believe robots could ever replace teachers — or will humans always be better at it?

1088. What three values do you think make a friendship strong and lasting?

1089. If a fly flew into your mouth, what would you do — panic, laugh, or drink water fast?

1090. Have you ever left a movie early because it just wasn't for you? What happened?

1091. If you had been on the Titanic, what would you have done to stay safe and find a lifeboat?

1092. Is there a favorite dish from another country you wish you could enjoy at home?

1093. What motto inspires you daily and helps guide your choices?

1094. Have you ever been somewhere that made you feel like you were standing at the edge of the world?

1095. Do you agree that love and war excuse all actions — or are there always rules to respect?

1096. Can you share a funny story about tossing or flipping pancakes?

1097. How many songs can you think of that mention numbers — like "One," "Two," or even "1999"?

1098. What's the most creative (or silly) thing you used to write something when no pen was nearby?

1099. Which movie would you love to see again but from a totally different character's point of view?

1100. What's the most touching or incredible thing you've seen an animal learn to do?

1101. If you could enhance or grow one part of yourself, what would you pick and why?

1102. What strange or funny thing do you think would happen if a vampire tried to bite a zombie?

1103. Have you ever flown a kite — and can you describe the last time you watched it soar?

1104. What's the most creative or funny car windshield sunshade you've ever seen?

1105. Do you think love at first sight is real — and has it ever happened to you?

1106. Do you panic at 20% battery — or are you calm until it's almost dead?

1107. Was there a life-changing moment for you when you knew you had crossed a point of no return?

1108. How would you define a meaningful, successful life beyond fame and fortune?

1109. If you could invent something to save you time each day, what would it do?

1110. What's your approach when someone tailgates you — stay calm, speed up, slow down, or something else?

1111. If you were 90% sure, would you risk losing $10,000 to try for $100,000?

1112. What unusual or funny name would you bet would never be chosen for a royal baby?

1113. How would you handle it if five people wanted one last slice of pizza?

1114. What little thing today annoyed you — even if you know it wasn't a big deal?

1115. Have you ever received a secret Valentine that stayed a mystery?

1116. If you had to name a racing dog, what name would you give it to make it sound fast and fun?

1117. Which celebrity's fame do you think did more harm than good?

1118. What world-changing event from your lifetime do you think will be in history books 100 years from now?

1119. Who's the person you feel has helped you most to become who you are today?

1120. What's a rule you feel very strongly about always keeping, no exceptions?

1121. What would be your first move to meet people and make friends in a new place?

1122. Imagine the three little pigs in a magical world — what strange things might they build houses with?

1123. When was your most recent snowball fight — and who did you have the snowy showdown with?

1124. What delicious signature bake would you showcase if you were a contestant?

1125. Do you have any jewelry or heirloom that used to belong to a family member?

1126. What's the weirdest thing you've ever slept on — maybe during an unexpected adventure?

1127. Have you ever whispered a wish to the stars — and did it come true?

1128. What song captures your spirit, your story, or your energy best?

1129. Imagine you get to name a brand-new month — what would you call it?

1130. What three things would you sacrifice today to get something your heart truly desires?

1131. How many steps do you usually take in a day — and do you have a step goal you try to reach?

1132. What silly or long team name would make it almost impossible for cheerleaders to shout or spell easily?

1133. Which person's life would you love to observe for a day to learn their secrets to handling life?

1134. What's the most recent thing you did where you felt super competitive?

1135. If you had an unlimited budget, what amazing place would you pick for dinner tonight?

1136. What things or moments make you feel soft-hearted, nostalgic, or extra emotional?

1137. Have you come across a word that's innocent in one country but hilarious or shocking in another?

1138. What's the best way you've heard someone turn a height joke into a confident, funny reply?

1139. Which friend brings huge energy and confidence everywhere they go?

1140. What pen name would you use if you became an author — something meaningful, fun, or mysterious?

1141. What major risk to humanity's future worries you most — and can we prevent it?

1142. Whose life story would you love to tell on the big screen by playing them?

1143. Can you share a fun or funny memory you have from relaxing in a hot tub?

1144. What fresh or bold color would you love to see on all the taxis in New York City?

1145. What's a word you love saying just because it sounds so joyful or funny?

1146. What happened the time (if ever) you forgot someone important's birthday?

1147. If you started a company to rival Amazon, what would be a catchy or funny name for it?

1148. Do you think being an only child is a loss — or does it offer a special kind of experience?

1149. If you had to name one of your little habits with a brand-new word, what would you call it?

1150. If you could spend a day inside a video game world, which one would you pick and why?

1151. What childhood game do you think has been forgotten by today's generation?

1152. Was there a moment you wished you could split yourself in two to be everywhere you wanted?

1153. What calming routines or tricks help you when you're having trouble sleeping?

1154. If you could take a special tour anywhere, what fascinating place would you choose and why?

1155. Have you ever dunked a biscuit into your tea? What's your verdict: delicious or messy?

1156. What craft, repair, or DIY project did you last dive into?

1157. How did you spend your last birthday — and what made it meaningful?

1158. What was the most magical monument or cityscape you've seen glowing at night?

1159. When was your most recent nosebleed — and did it happen somewhere unexpected?

1160. If someone kept stealing food from your plate, what playful punishment would you dream up?

1161. If you had to pick a thirst-quenching drink besides water, what would it be?

1162. What's a recent win you proudly bragged about — even just a little?

1163. If Lego asked you to design a brand-new set, what would your creation look like?

1164. Which superpower would you rather not have — and why would it be more trouble than it's worth?

1165. If Atlantis were real, where would you bet it's hidden — under the ocean, desert, or somewhere else?

1166. What would your dream version of paradise include — from people to places to feelings?

1167. Can you create a motivational sportswear slogan that's even better than "Just do it"?

1168. What five items would you place in a time capsule to capture today's world for people 25 years from now?

1169. What would you do differently if you had to pedal a bike to power your home each day?

1170. How would you react if you saw an angry elephant coming right at you?

1171. What's a time you discovered you were the last person to know about something big?

1172. What is the loudest sound you remember hearing — where were you?

1173. If you had jury duty for a huge case, would you stay or try to avoid it?

1174. When was the last time you donated to or bought something from a thrift store?

1175. Who in your life is like a never-ending fountain of creative or wild ideas?

1176. What's your favorite treat to grab for an afternoon pick-me-up?

1177. What's in your pockets right now — and do you always carry the same things?

1178. What new, fun, or helpful feature do you imagine future cars will have?

1179. What cause would move you enough to take to the streets for a peaceful protest?

1180. When do you feel the deepest pride in your home country?

1181. Have you ever found yourself laughing after bumping your funny bone?

1182. What's your go-to food that comes on a stick, from fairs or festivals?

1183. Would you hitch a ride from a stranger if you had no phone and were stuck?

1184. What's the most epic hold-wait you've had to survive on the phone?

1185. How many things are always plugged in at your place — even when you're not using them?

1186. If you notice someone walking out of a restroom with paper on their shoe, what do you do?

1187. Do you think jousting should make a comeback as an official Olympic sport?

1188. What's a time when a DIY remedy or treatment at home hilariously didn't work out?

1189. What local treat or meal is your hometown famous for?

1190. What treasure, place, or memory do you believe is lost forever?

1191. On your 90th birthday, which family members do you dream of celebrating with?

1192. If you could receive a signed photo from someone you admire, who would you choose?

1193. If you got to name a future storm, what creative name would you pick?

1194. If you had to rebrand the Smurfs with a new name, what would you call them?

1195. What's the funniest or weirdest mistake you've made while singing along to a song?

1196. Did you leave cookies, milk, or carrots out for Santa and his reindeer growing up?

1197. What's the cleverest identical twin prank you've ever come across?

1198. If you could win gold in an Olympic swim race, which stroke would you choose?

1199. If you could wave a magic wand and change three things about your job, what would they be?

1200. Who did you last surprise with flowers, and what made you choose to do it?

1201. If Yankee Doodle wanted something different in his cap, what fun item would it be?

1202. Have you ever spent a morning believing a crazy dream you had actually happened?

1203. If you could design a candy heart with your own phrase, what would it say?

1204. If you were buried by snow in an avalanche, what would you try to do first to survive?

1205. Which of Snow White's seven dwarfs do you feel you are most like?

1206. Have you ever seen a hilarious or brilliant license plate? What did it say?

1207. Have you ever had a friend or coworker who used way too much "tech talk" for simple things?

1208. If you could experience one beautiful moment again for the first time, what would it be?

1209. Has anyone ever told you something that made you wish you could "unhear" it?

1210. How do you gracefully manage when you forget someone's name right before an introduction?

1211. Have you ever heard of a job that sounds completely bizarre but really exists?

1212. What's something you accidentally erased or deleted that made you frustrated?

1213. If you needed to replace your right foot with an animal's foot, which animal would you pick?

1214. If you could repeat one special, once-in-a-lifetime experience, which one would it be?

1215. Who do you think wears the crown for being the biggest pop star of all time?

1216. If you could create a new emoji for your phone, what would it be and how would you use it?

1217. If you could have one promise that could never be broken, what would you want it to be?

1218. Imagine a Hogwarts from a different world — what would it be the school of?

1219. Do you believe in fate guiding our lives? Why or why not?

1220. How do you excuse yourself when someone is talking non-stop?

1221. If your body could warn people with a silly sound like a rattlesnake, what part would buzz?

1222. What's the biggest haircut disaster you've survived?

1223. What strange combo of talents would make a show you'd definitely watch?

1224. What movie do you know by heart because you've seen it so many times?

1225. Which TV ad touched your heart so much it made you cry?

1226. What were you doing the last time you got really sweaty?

1227. Imagine a world without music — how would it change your life?

1228. What uplifting or inspiring note would you want someone to find inside their chocolate?

1229. If you could disguise something ordinary as a spy gadget, what would you turn it into?

1230. What universal hand signal or gesture can you think of that almost anyone would understand?

1231. Would you be brave enough to pet a cockroach, or would you run away?

1232. What's the last thing you canceled, and did it make you feel relieved or disappointed?

1233. Is there a special seat at home that everyone knows belongs to a certain someone?

1234. What's something you were reminded of recently that you'd prefer not to remember?

1235. If you could be stuck in an elevator with a celebrity, who would make it a fun or memorable time?

1236. What's the longest or most memorable bridge you've ever gone over?

1237. Should giving back be mandatory for the very wealthy? Why or why not?

1238. Have you ever gone a long time without talking to someone important to you? What happened?

1239. If you had to run from something scary, how far would you make it before stopping?

1240. What Guinness World Record would you secretly (or proudly) love to have?

1241. Do you believe that happiness can be chosen, even on tough days?

1242. Can you remember a handmade gift you received that meant a lot to you?

1243. If you could rename The Lion, the Witch and the Wardrobe for a different world, what would it be?

1244. What keys do you still depend on, and which key would be a nightmare to lose?

1245. What's the weirdest thing you've seen someone carrying on their car roof?

1246. At what number of children do you think a family starts feeling a little overwhelming?

1247. What fun or yummy jelly bean flavor would you like to invent?

1248. If sneezing triggered a little song, what would your sneeze theme be?

1249. What little thing always cheers you up the moment you see it?

1250. Do you find live music more magical at outdoor events? Why?

1251. What do you do to wake up when you're feeling really sleepy in the morning?

1252. Have you ever gone to the theater alone, and what was the experience like for you?

1253. If you were gifted any piece of dream jewelry, what would it be and why?

1254. Who would you secretly love to have a playful water pistol fight with?

1255. What's the most precious file on your computer or device you'd be devastated to lose?

1256. Have you ever gotten into mischief or trouble just because you were too curious?

1257. Which Google Doodle made you smile or left an impression on you?

1258. If you were taken in by mistake, what would be the "crime" you'd most likely be blamed for?

1259. What sweet or meaningful verse would you write for a special greeting card?

1260. Which fun old slang word deserves a comeback today?

1261. If you could wish something wonderful for someone else, what would it be?

1262. Which three kinds of things do you never buy without making sure they have good reviews?

1263. Can you remember your very first cellphone? What brand was it?

1264. If you could live in space for six months, would you do it or stay on Earth?

1265. When did you last stand up for someone who couldn't stand up for themselves?

1266. If you had to rename Nike today, what powerful new name would you choose?

1267. What's a funny or inspiring memory you have from a workout or exercise class?

1268. Have you ever overheard or found out something you wish you hadn't? What happened?

1269. What gadget do you love using the most for taking photos?

1270. If you went missing, who do you believe would miss you the most deeply?

1271. What funny movie never fails to crack you up, even on the worst days?

1272. If someone gave you $1,000 but you had to spend it within an hour, what would you get?

1273. What style of jeans do you reach for first when you want to feel great?

1274. If you had to pick the worst possible moment and place for a loud fart, what would it be?

1275. If you could outlaw one thing just for a day, what would you choose?

1276. When was the last time you felt a jolt of excitement or fear — and why?

1277. If Harry Houdini had kept performing, what thrilling escape act would you imagine he'd attempt?

1278. What's a situation or decision you feel almost always ends badly?

1279. What's the funniest or most wrong version of your name someone has used?

1280. Can you remember the last time you made up a funny or personal hashtag?

1281. What three adorable or creative names would you give to baby penguins?

1282. When you win at something, what's a fun phrase you'd like to shout out instead of "who's the daddy?"

1283. What's the ideal age for someone to retire and start a new chapter?

1284. What comforting winter food would feel strange to eat in the summer?

1285. What dreamy, cozy, or fun scent would you love to turn into a candle?

1286. If your feet grew bigger every time you thought about a snack today, what size would they be?

1287. What made you feel so surprised, happy, or emotional that you couldn't find the words?

1288. What's the first thing you notice about someone you find beautiful?

1289. Have you ever felt silly after winning a debate, realizing you were wrong all along?

1290. What funny or fitting consequence should happen to people who hog the freeway's middle lane?

1291. Do you have a friend or family member who can do funny tricks like wiggling their ears?

1292. Is there something you think is harmless but still gives you the icks to touch?

1293. What's the best treasure you've ever found hidden away in your clothes?

1294. What's the last thing you recommended that you think everyone should try?

1295. Which Little Miss or Mr. Men character reminds you most of yourself?

1296. What comforting or exciting meal would you want on your plate every Wednesday?

1297. What playful version of chess pieces would make the game even more fun for you?

1298. Would you try walking over hot coals for the challenge and adventure of it?

1299. If you could make a brand-new encyclopedia, what would it be filled with?

1300. Did you ever get detention at school, and what did you do to earn it?

1301. If you had to pick a song for CPR timing, what beat would you keep in mind?

1302. Should kids be protected from loot boxes in games, or is it part of gaming fun?

1303. Tell me about a special or funny memory you have from a high-end restaurant.

1304. Is there something you've sworn never to taste, no matter how adventurous you feel?

1305. Have you heard of anything heartwarming or shocking caught by a hidden nanny cam?

1306. How much more expensive do you think it would be to recreate the Six Million Dollar Man today?

1307. When you see a single shoe on the side of the street, what story pops into your head?

1308. Would you prefer to write your life story yourself, or have someone else capture it for you?

1309. What would you do if you saw someone sitting and crying outside?

1310. If you noticed someone sneaking food into their bag without paying, what would you do?

1311. Has anyone ever told you that you inspired or helped them like a hero? What happened?

1312. How do you handle people talking when you're trying to enjoy a movie at the cinema?

1313. If you wrote a loving poem about a food you adore, what food would you choose?

1314. What's the last time you burned your fingers on something too hot?

1315. Which spray-on item (perfume, air freshener, etc.) has a scent you love most?

1316. What's something you think might be banned soon, whether serious or silly?

1317. If you could give dollar bills a whole new makeover, what design would you create?

1318. Which Jungle Book character would you love to have as a friend?

1319. If you could choose any voice to guide you on GPS, whose voice would it be?

1320. Which school subject challenged you the most, and how did you cope?

1321. How many books do you typically get through in a year?

1322. If a robber wanted to make people laugh, what silly mask should they wear?

1323. If you could design a magical new ice cream flavor, what would you choose?

1324. What feels truly special the first time but not as much afterward?

1325. When was the last time you were so confused you didn't know what to do?

1326. What are the signs that a steak has been cooked just the way you like it?

1327. If you could give goats new names instead of billy and nanny, what would they be?

1328. What comment would be an absolute disaster to say during a wedding ceremony?

1329. What else would be fun or convenient to have packaged in a bag like tea bags?

1330. What uplifting news story recently gave you hope or happiness?

1331. What little upgrade would you give people if you could redesign the human body?

1332. What's the funniest thing you've ever seen used like a musical instrument?

1333. Which holiday could use a refresh to make it feel exciting again?

1334. What would you attempt if you felt completely fearless about falling?

1335. What beautiful or relaxing name would you give a spa for women?

1336. What's your most memorable hair or beauty fail?

1337. Who were you rocking out with the last time you had a Bohemian Rhapsody moment?

1338. What's a home remedy for constipation you've heard of — or even tried?

1339. Can people really change, or are they who they are forever?

1340. When's the last time you did something and immediately regretted it?

1341. How would your friendships and routines feel different without cell phones?

1342. What's a dinosaur fact that you find super interesting or fun?

1343. When was the worst sunburn you've ever had, and what happened?

1344. What do you do if someone gets too close for comfort without realizing it?

1345. If you had to trade fingers with a friend for a day, who would you trust?

1346. What magic trick totally amazed you the first time you saw it?

1347. Would your friends turn to you when things go wrong or an emergency strikes?

1348. How would you adapt your routine if you could only use one arm for a whole day?

1349. What's one anti-aging secret you've heard about and thought was worth trying?

1350. What's a meaningful or fun tradition your family keeps alive?

1351. What inspiring or beautiful thing have you seen crafted from recycled materials?

1352. Have you ever chosen to take a cold shower, and how did it make you feel?

1353. What signs of nature make you smile because you know spring is near?

1354. If you were born on February 29, how would you choose your birthday most years?

1355. Are there any professional athletes you feel earn more than they deserve?

1356. What was your highest-ever score on a test, and what was it for?

1357. If magic beans grew into something other than a giant beanstalk, what would you hope for?

1358. How long have you stayed completely indoors without going outside?

1359. If you could contribute one important word to a book about life, what would it be?

1360. How do you react when someone approaches you for help or money in public?

1361. If you had to create a new word for a yawn-burp combo, what would you call it?

1362. What's the longest you've stayed awake — and why didn't you sleep?

1363. Can you name a few bones in the human body without looking it up?

1364. What's a little everyday thing that always fills your heart with beauty?

1365. When did you last enjoy the simple feeling of the wind in your hair?

1366. What's the most fun or silly color you've ever worn as pants?

1367. If you could turn towels into fun origami animals or shapes, what would you choose?

1368. What's a powerful or eye-opening thing you discovered through a documentary?

1369. Where do you go — in real life or your imagination — to find new ideas?

1370. What's the most loving or thoughtful thing someone has ever done just for you?

1371. If you could dream up a magical or cozy theme for a hotel room, what would it be?

1372. When you have something exciting to share, who's the first person you think of?

1373. What's something you know in your heart you're naturally good at?

1374. Have you ever had such a bad experience that you gave it a zero rating?

1375. What's a pizza topping that you just can't believe people actually like?

1376. Which teacher do you remember struggling with the most, and why?

1377. What's the bravest or most adventurous thing you've dared to do?

1378. Do you pay attention to how many times you chew before you eat?

1379. What's a food combo your friends like that you just can't stomach?

1380. What were your favorite songs or games to pass time on car journeys growing up?

1381. Can you remember a time when a plan sounded amazing but totally backfired?

1382. What's something you find simple that lots of other people find hard?

1383. What's your most hilarious or fun bounce house adventure?

1384. Do you believe in unidentified flying objects? Have you had a strange experience?

1385. What's the worst time you got stuck in traffic — and what event were you trying to reach?

1386. If your hair had an animal twin instead of a ponytail, what would it be?

1387. Which three words describe the feeling of falling truly, beautifully in love?

1388. When did you end up being the center of attention, even though you didn't want to be?

1389. What's something that made you say "aww" because it was just so cute?

1390. Do you believe life events have meaning behind them, or are they random?

1391. If you could invent a silly or fun rule for marathon runners, what would it be?

1392. Imagine you're a master thief — what's the most amazing thing you would have stolen?

1393. What's something you did recently that you usually get annoyed at others for doing?

1394. How often do you find yourself reaching for your phone without thinking?

1395. Which device in your house burns through batteries the fastest?

1396. If you had to invent a meal with only what's in your fridge right now, what would it be?

1397. What new clothing combo would you invent to be stylish and fun?

1398. What moments remind you that life is too rich to be just a simulation?

1399. Can focusing your mind really change what happens around you?

1400. What health advice would you never follow, even if it's supposed to be good for you?

1401. Have you ever had a bad hunch that turned out to be true?

1402. What interrupts your concentration the most when you're focused on a task?

1403. Have you ever been banned or unwelcome somewhere? Why?

1404. If you could teach a parrot to say something sweet or funny, what would it be?

1405. Is there always something positive to find in hard situations?

1406. What's the most unexpected thing you've poked your own eye with by accident?

1407. When did you last enjoy walking barefoot in the sand?

1408. If you created a brand-new shape, what would it be called and why?

1409. Who do you know that makes blowing their nose a full concert performance?

1410. What creative charity challenge would you design that people would love to join?

1411. What simple thing could happen today that would make you smile even more?

1412. What delicious dessert from your family would you make sure gets passed down?

1413. What's something funny or creative you've done just to get some "me time"?

1414. Would marriage feel different if you had to renew it each year like a subscription?

1415. Which character from Thomas the Tank Engine do you relate to the most?

1416. Who's got tattoos you find really stylish or inspiring?

1417. What inspiring or funny story has an older person told you?

1418. Do you find sleeping with socks cozy or uncomfortable?

1419. What funny or adorable shape would you trim a big green bush into?

1420. If you were in a wheelbarrow race, would you want to steer or be pushed?

1421. What's the most unusual or hilarious thing you've heard someone ask a famous person to sign?

1422. If you could dream up a family board game, what three fun ideas would you include?

1423. What topic caught your curiosity and made you spend forever reading on Wikipedia?

1424. Who was your first kiss with, and what do you remember most about it?

1425. Which of your habits would be hardest to quit even if you wanted to?

1426. What sport or physical activity at school made you happiest?

1427. How many times do you think you've looked in a mirror today without even realizing?

1428. What warm meal would you miss the most if you could never eat hot food again?

1429. What's the most "high-up" place you've ever traveled to?

1430. Do you have a getting-dressed ritual you always stick to?

1431. What's a deep or funny question that might never ever have an answer?

1432. What foods have funny or weird names that don't match what they really are?

1433. Are you more of a Coke fan or a Pepsi fan — and why do you feel that fits you?

1434. What's the sweetest or funniest babysitting moment you remember?

1435. As a little kid, did you ever push something silly up your nose or into your ear?

1436. What's something in your life that feels priceless and can't be bought?

1437. If you could watch only one TV channel from now on, which would it be?

1438. What animal would be even cuter or cooler if it had colorful stripes?

1439. Have you ever asked for a hairstyle because a celebrity had it?

1440. Which movie's story feels unfinished and deserves a great sequel?

1441. What's the coolest or most joyful celebration dance you've ever watched?

1442. What games did you play at school that are now considered too dangerous?

1443. What's the most exciting prize you've ever won?

1444. Which "deadly sin" (like pride, envy, or laziness) is your biggest challenge?

1445. If you had to come up with a reason the Earth might be flat, what funny argument would you make?

1446. What three words would your friends use to describe how you dress or express yourself?

1447. If you could pick a place to be remembered forever, where would your ashes go?

1448. What's a piece of advice that helped shape who you are today?

1449. What would be the silliest or least practical outfit you could wear for a field day?

1450. Who was the girl everyone admired at your school, and why do you think that was?

1451. What's the messiest thing you ever spilled or dropped in public?

1452. If you didn't pass your driving test the first few times, how determined would you be to keep trying?

1453. What celebrity would be your nightmare partner for a ballroom dance?

1454. When you hear creaks and bumps after dark, what do you secretly think they might be?

1455. What playful new image could mean "it's the end" instead of the usual old sayings?

1456. What's something you tried recently that you quickly realized was a bad idea?

1457. Which online influencer inspires you or shares a message you connect with?

1458. What spread or topping makes toast the best comfort food for you?

1459. What would you do if you came back after a swim and your shoes were missing?

1460. What's the weirdest or most creative hot dog topping you've heard of?

1461. Have you ever used a key to wind something up? What was it?

1462. What's something super rare that you'd love to see in real life?

1463. When did you last do something brave that felt totally unfamiliar?

1464. What would be the grossest or weirdest surprise to find in an old coat pocket?

1465. How many projects have you left half-done lately?

1466. What funny or crazy changes could you imagine for Snow White's world?

1467. When was a time you felt unfairly blamed for something you didn't do?

1468. What's the furthest north and furthest south you've gone on a trip?

1469. What rule or privilege should be available to younger people?

1470. What's one item you'd love even more if it came in your favorite color?

1471. What inspiring catchphrase would you give Greta Thunberg for her climate work?

1472. Which grounded animal would be stunning or magical if it could fly?

1473. If you were homebound forever, what freedom or place would you miss most?

1474. Which instrument sounds the most emotional or tearful to you?

1475. Have you ever tried to sneak around but ended up making a huge noise?

1476. How much of your country's anthem can you sing from memory?

1477. What's your best trick for getting a noisy classroom or party full of kids to listen?

1478. Would you parent and set boundaries like your parents did, or take a different path?

1479. What's something silly you did recently that you hope no one caught on camera?

1480. What's something fun or silly Jack and Jill could have gone to get up the hill?

1481. What's one feature of your face you love and wouldn't change?

1482. What would you miss most if you had no internet at all?

1483. What food would you steer clear of on a date because it could get messy?

1484. When did you last feel amazing, proud, and on top of everything?

1485. What hilarious animal would be a silly replacement for Pony Express ponies?

1486. Which TV series would you miss the most if you could never watch again?

1487. Who would be a fun and mysterious new suspect to add to Clue?

1488. Which magazine did you love enough to get a subscription for?

1489. Which album has every song you absolutely love?

1490. Which slang word has found a permanent spot in your everyday talk?

1491. Are you quick to name a song after hearing the first few seconds?

1492. When did you learn the hard way that a "freebie" wasn't really free?

1493. Which two creatures would make the funniest race like the tortoise and the hare?

1494. What meaningful thing do you wish you had that money can't purchase?

1495. What would you do with a million-dollar donation to make the world better?

1496. Which chocolate do you always grab first when picking from a fancy box?

1497. If you could only walk backward for 24 hours, when would it be most awkward?

1498. What silly subject would make a hilarious Ed Sheeran song?

1499. When you were little, what age did you think was super old?

1500. Have you ever helped an animal in need? Tell the story!

1501. When during the day do you feel your happiest?

1502. What are three things you could happily declutter from your home right now?

1503. What catchy song has you humming without realizing it?

1504. Do you think remembering people in harder times helps you feel more thankful?

1505. What quote would make an amazing motto for a shoe brand?

1506. Have you ever missed a joke while everyone else was laughing? What happened?

1507. What's something nice you recently did for yourself just because you deserved it?

1508. How many times do you boil the kettle to make your favorite drinks each day?

1509. What super annoying but non-harmful thing would be great for mild "torture"?

1510. Which song sounded so fun until you realized what it was actually about?

1511. Which famous person would you love to have as your personal mentor?

1512. Is there someone you've disliked for a long time — and could that ever change?

1513. Is there ever an age limit for showing off your best street dance moves?

1514. What playground favorite deserves a spot at the Olympics?

1515. What funny or unbelievable tale did your grandparents pass down to you?

1516. What waiting music makes you want to hang up immediately?

1517. Do you think balloon releases should be banned to help nature and wildlife?

1518. What GIF did you last send that captured exactly how you felt?

1519. Imagine a brand new cheese with a silly name — what would you call it?

1520. What new thing, big or small, are you grateful to have today that you didn't a year ago?

1521. What's your memory of eating with chopsticks for the first time?

1522. Which myth would you most like to prove is either true or totally false?

1523. Can you think of someone who let a tiny bit of power make them act differently?

1524. Have you ever found a hidden gem that someone else tossed out?

1525. If you wrote a song lyric starting with "She had jet-black hair," what would your next line be?

1526. How would you make sure people think twice before littering?

1527. What food would you be saddest to give up if you couldn't chew anymore?

1528. Which friend makes you laugh (or cringe) at how they eat at the table?

1529. What names were super trendy the year you arrived in the world?

1530. If everyone flushed at the same time, what crazy thing do you think would happen?

1531. Which store would you pick to get a $500 shopping spree?

1532. What was the last movie you saw at the theater and who did you go with?

1533. What technology we use today will people laugh at in the future?

1534. What's the craziest plant you've come across?

1535. What handy extra would you love to see built into a wristwatch?

1536. If you had to wait for hours in an elevator, what food would you crave most?

1537. What three things make a woman instantly warm and likable to others?

1538. If given $50 to lift someone's spirits, how would you use it?

1539. In a zombie world, what skill would help you stay alive the longest?

1540. What fun or silly pose did you hold during the mannequin challenge?

1541. If scientists found something unbelievable on Mars, what do you think it could be?

1542. When was the last time you knew you made someone's day or life better?

1543. What's something that's not banned but would seem scary on a plane?

1544. During a scary, stormy night, would you dare to answer the door?

1545. As a little girl, what did you name your two favorite toys?

1546. What was the last thing you downloaded, and why did you pick it?

1547. If you had to have an animal's teeth for a day, whose teeth would you pick?

1548. What's something you've done that helped improve someone's life?

1549. Have you ever been so joyful that you cried happy tears?

1550. Does the idea of robots ruling the world ever scare you?

1551. What's your favorite dollar store find ever?

1552. Have you ever headed to work or school still wearing yesterday's undies?

1553. What job do you think is underappreciated but super important?

1554. How much money would make you feel content and free?

1555. What's something silly or funny you did when you were exhausted?

1556. What flavor do you always notice, even if it's mixed into other foods?

1557. What would you create for a gluten-free, vegan-friendly lunch?

1558. If you created a spooky plant, what name would you call it?

1559. What little accomplishment always makes you feel proud?

1560. What playful comparison could you use instead of "old as the hills"?

1561. What heartfelt advice would you give your younger self at ten years old?

1562. Has anyone said you remind them of a famous woman? Who?

1563. What's the most disgusting thing you've seen floating in a jar?

1564. When was the last time someone made you want to scream, and what happened?

1565. What food would you wish people wouldn't eat near others in tight places?

1566. Do you think every question deserves respect, even if it sounds silly?

1567. What's something you love even more than cats love fitting into boxes?

1568. Have you ever tried cooking an egg on a hot car surface?

1569. What's the cleverest lazy thing you've ever seen someone do?

1570. What cloud number would you float on instead of Cloud Nine?

1571. If you could design fun medals for a parallel Olympics, what would they be?

1572. Who's the last person you went to visit in a hospital?

1573. What natural scene took your breath away the most?

1574. Is there a kind of music that really isn't your vibe?

1575. What's the key thing that keeps a relationship healthy?

1576. Who's your moodiest friend, and how do you lift their spirits?

1577. How would you help both endangered animals and plants survive together?

1578. What sweet or bold rhyme would you pair with "looking at the sun"?

1579. What's the worst neighbor story you've lived through?

1580. If you had to buy just one new clothing item each year, what would it be?

1581. What delicious or surprising potato chip flavor would you invent?

1582. Can you list bands that have a number in their name?

1583. What funny thing would you bury to trick future explorers?

1584. Have you ever had a fun night at a drive-in movie?

1585. What's something you underestimated and found really tough?

1586. How much money would make you walk away from work for good?

1587. What inspiring speech or beautiful poem would you want to memorize?

1588. When was your last fireworks experience, and where did it happen?

1589. What show or movie surprised you because you found it by accident?

1590. Who in your family loves tea the most and knows all about it?

1591. What's the most unusual way you've gotten from one place to another?

1592. If drafted in WWI, would you have gone to war or protested it?

1593. What creative or funny ways have you seen parents try to get babies to sleep?

1594. Have you ever used a nickname for someone that felt a little mean?

1595. What's the gentlest or softest thing you've ever felt?

1596. When was the last time someone leaned on you for support?

1597. Is there a "weird" food you love but rarely tell others about?

1598. How big of a head start would you need to reach your bathroom before a sprinting Usain Bolt?

1599. What was the most uncomfortable outfit you wore for style's sake?

1600. Which college program do you think makes finding a job hardest?

1601. What strange excuse did you hear that ended up being completely true?

1602. If bananas came in a different shape, what shape would you like?

1603. When you were ten, what was your regular bedtime?

1604. If the lights went out on a Saturday night, how would you keep yourself entertained?

1605. Which hairstyle from the past makes you wish you could hide the pictures?

1606. How would you gently peel off a really stuck bandage?

1607. Can you think of something you dreaded recently but ended up handling well?

1608. After seeing Jaws, did you ever feel nervous around water?

1609. What's something you love most about who you are?

1610. In a one-minute shower, which parts would be your top priority?

1611. Who in your family or circle has the most famously stinky feet?

1612. As a child, what funny names did you have for everyday things?

1613. What's something you did that you really regret now?

1614. Why do you think people say "crime never pays"? Do you agree?

1615. Which drone photo has totally amazed you recently?

1616. Have you ever pretended to like something someone showed you but found it super creepy?

1617. What fun color would you love toilet paper to come in?

1618. When was the last time luck helped you in a big or small way?

1619. What's the prettiest or funniest balloon animal or thing you've seen?

1620. What everyday thing would be hardest to do if you wore clown shoes?

1621. What handy tool do you think a Swiss army knife is missing?

1622. What healthy or cozy dish would you make with lentils as the focus?

1623. What knock-knock joke always makes you laugh?

1624. What fun and empowering events would you add to a "ladies' Olympics" at work?

1625. Which quote inspires you to follow your dreams even when it's tough?

1626. Would you support a law making organ donation the standard for saving lives?

1627. What event made you buy tickets months before it happened?

1628. What cartoon from your childhood got a reboot that disappointed you?

1629. What's the funniest silly story someone ever made up about you?

1630. What magical or beautiful name would you give your dragon?

1631. What's one change that would help you grow into the woman you dream of being?

1632. If you stopped flying, how would it affect seeing loved ones or traveling for fun?

1633. If you could create a "Hall of Kindness," who would you honor first?

1634. Aside from diamonds, what do you personally consider to be your most loyal or dependable companion?

1635. Have you ever heard a sass-filled or smart one-liner that made you laugh?

1636. Imagine a wall decorated with something unexpected—what would you choose to stick on it?

1637. Can you think of a moment when someone else ended up being right about something?

1638. When was the last time you wanted to lash out but chose not to?

1639. What type of hat would feel most like your signature look if you wore it daily?

1640. Have you ever created something from scratch that made you feel proud? What was it?

1641. Picture a dramatic novel where the tiniest creatures rule the world—what would you call it?

1642. Whose sneeze always makes you laugh because it's so dramatic or unique?

1643. Which musical act with a color in their name do you enjoy most, and what memory does it bring up?

1644. What childhood toy of yours would make a perfect animated sidekick?

1645. If your voice could magically take on a dreamy or classy accent, what would it be?

1646. What personal truth or mindset do you now accept that younger you wouldn't have understood?

1647. Would you feel brave or terrified if you were asked to help land a plane in a crisis?

1648. If you had to name an all-female tribute band for a famous artist, what would you call it?

1649. What tiny award or compliment in your school days made you feel proud inside?

1650. Which treat do you love and hate at the same time—and wish you had a reason to stop eating?

1651. What color would you wear most often if it meant ease, comfort, and style in one tee?

1652. What little frustration had you venting like your life depended on it?

1653. Have you ever planted something tiny and watched it bloom? How did it feel?

1654. What's a special place in your area that people travel for, but you rarely visit?

1655. What skin-care lesson from your teen years would you pass on to the next generation?

1656. If you could design your own jelly bean color and taste, what would it be?

1657. Imagine cash printed on something soft or stylish—what fabric would you choose?

1658. Do you collect anything small or beautiful that brings you joy when you see it?

1659. What's the one meal you always reach for the salt shaker before tasting?

1660. Do you ever still use a house phone? What was your last call about?

1661. What meal wouldn't feel right without a generous side of ketchup?

1662. Imagine riding off into the sunset—who would be holding your hand?

1663. In your thriller story, where's the most unexpected spot a clue could be buried?

1664. What's a special place in your area that people travel for, but you rarely visit?

1665. What skin-care lesson from your teen years would you pass on to the next generation?

1666. If you could design your own jelly bean color and taste, what would it be?

1667. Imagine cash printed on something soft or stylish—what fabric would you choose?

1668. Do you collect anything small or beautiful that brings you joy when you see it?

1669. What's the one meal you always reach for the salt shaker before tasting?

1670. Do you ever still use a house phone? What was your last call about?

1671. What meal wouldn't feel right without a generous side of ketchup?

1672. Imagine riding off into the sunset—who would be holding your hand?

1673. In your thriller story, where's the most unexpected spot a clue could be buried?

1674. What's your go-to comfort ritual when you feel emotionally drained?

1675. What type of product would feel the most awkward for you to promote?

1676. What silly story did you believe growing up that turned out to be totally made up?

1677. Have you ever been confused by a familiar product that had a strange name overseas?

1678. When's the last time someone surprised you and made your whole day better?

1679. Which flavor of chips would you stockpile if it was the only one left in the world?

1680. What message on a shirt made you stop and smile (or roll your eyes)?

1681. Did you have a black-eyeliner-and-bangs phase—or know someone who rocked that vibe?

1682. Which childhood tale character do you secretly relate to more than you'd admit?

1683. If you could blink and be at your destination, how would you use your extra time?

1684. What fashion, hairstyle, or pop trend were you not allowed to join in growing up?

1685. If women got to rename "pants" for everyone to use, what would your word be?

1686. How do you keep your earbuds neat and easy to find in your bag or purse?

1687. If your personality was a T-shirt quote, what would it be?

1688. Who's the woman in your life you always carve out time for, no matter what?

1689. What heartfelt or practical questions would you enjoy answering for others?

1690. Which sausage do you secretly love—on toast, in pasta, or at brunch?

1691. What photo did you last text someone—maybe something personal, cute, or funny?

1692. Who was the girl that made everyone laugh—and did you have a moment like that?

1693. What object would you take with you that's full of meaning or memories?

1694. What keepsake or gift with your name on it holds special meaning for you?

1695. Think back to your first girls' night in. Who came and what do you remember most?

1696. What's the most packed place you've ever been—concerts, festivals, or travel moments?

1697. How often do you freshen up your space with color or décor changes?

1698. Have you had a dinner where everything went wrong but turned into a story worth telling?

1699. Who's the queen of drama in your world—and how do you navigate their emotions?

1700. Which food looks great on Instagram but is a pain to actually eat?

1701. What cheeky or silly term would you come up with for a sneeze + toot combo?

1702. What dream or goal are you slowly building a savings fund for?

1703. What classic or homemade extras make your roast dinners complete?

1704. Have you followed your intuition even when a rule said otherwise?

1705. What's a fair but funny way to deal with someone who drinks from the carton?

1706. What all-girl or co-ed bands with four members did you grow up listening to?

1707. Did you repair anything recently—at home, in your wardrobe, or emotionally?

1708. Ever gotten a black eye from a clumsy moment or while protecting someone?

1709. Would you be Elaine or someone with her sass in the Seinfeld world?

1710. Have you ever prepped a pineapple the easy way? What's your method?

1711. If you had a boat, what beautiful or quirky name would suit it?

1712. Do you tend to soften your words or speak your truth in sensitive situations?

1713. What words do you love to say when clinking glasses at a celebration?

1714. Have you followed your intuition even when a rule said otherwise?

1715. What's a fair but funny way to deal with someone who drinks from the carton?

1716. What all-girl or co-ed bands with four members did you grow up listening to?

1717. Did you repair anything recently—at home, in your wardrobe, or emotionally?

1718. Ever gotten a black eye from a clumsy moment or while protecting someone?

1719. Would you be Elaine or someone with her sass in the Seinfeld world?

1720. Have you ever prepped a pineapple the easy way? What's your method?

1721. If you had a boat, what beautiful or quirky name would suit it?

1722. Do you tend to soften your words or speak your truth in sensitive situations?

1723. What words do you love to say when clinking glasses at a celebration?

1724. What is one survey or poll that completely caught you off guard?

1725. What online class have you enjoyed the most, and why did you choose it?

1726. What is your go-to way to make hot chocolate feel comforting and indulgent?

1727. What are five places around the world that would be dream trips if nothing held you back?

1728. What instrument sound instantly makes you want to cover your ears?

1729. If you magically moved six feet over right now, what would you be landing on?

1730. Do you carry any charms or follow little rituals for good luck?

1731. Have you ever had a nickname that made you laugh or feel special?

1732. What is a recent moment this month that made you smile from the heart?

1733. What moment recently had you giving a spontaneous high-five?

1734. How would you handle an unexpected delivery that feels a little suspicious?

1735. Who are the two people—on screen or in real life—who crack you up together?

1736. What moment made you truly believe your mom had supernatural awareness?

1737. What adjustments would bring you more balance, peace, or confidence in life?

1738. Is there something you do so awkwardly that it's become part of your charm?

1739. What comforts or rituals do you miss most when you're away from home?

1740. When did you last stand your ground in a conversation—and how did it go?

1741. What song would you belt out confidently in front of a fun, supportive crowd?

1742. Who in your family gets lovingly teased for their driving "adventures"?

1743. Which chair in your home would you protect at all costs during a move—and why?

1744. What's the one nurturing dish you remember your mom making when you weren't feeling well?

1745. What's your most hilarious post-shower scramble when you realized you forgot a towel?

1746. Have you had a "small world" moment that made you gasp or laugh?

1747. Which movie quote do you love using to make people smile or roll their eyes?

1748. Have you ever connected with someone through letters alone? What did that feel like?

1749. What's your secret "mom trick" for getting medicine down with zero drama?

1750. Who's your built-in safety net when you're at home alone?

1751. Is there a truth that your heart isn't ready to carry—even if your head is?

1752. Do video reviews in sports make it feel more fair—or more frustrating?

1753. What do you think every young woman should leave school knowing how to do?

1754. If you wrote a whimsical book for kids about a charming hen, what would her name be?

1755. What's a meaningful insight you've shared with friends that was once shared with you?

1756. What everyday item would you love to turn into a sculpture like Stonehenge?

1757. If you peeked out of your tent and saw strange footprints, what animal would freak you out most?

1758. If you ruled a peaceful little country, what would your coins or bills be called?

1759. What look, word, or trend do you wish would stay in the past already?

1760. What would you do if someone you care about did something seriously wrong?

1761. Do you remember the last time you locked eyes in a stare battle—did you win or giggle first?

1762. What graceful or powerful creature should join the zodiac lineup?

1763. How often do you change your phone case to match your mood or outfit?

1764. What goodbye still lingers in your heart when you think back to it?

1765. Was there ever a trend you tried on but just couldn't take yourself seriously in?

1766. What cleaning tip has worked wonders for your windows or mirrors?

1767. If you had to rename Gorilla Glue after another animal, what name would sound fun and powerful?

1768. Which series is your go-to guilty pleasure, the one you always carve out time for?

1769. Have you found yourself doing something you once said you'd never, ever do?

1770. Which friend or relative always thinks they're seriously ill—and what's the wildest "self-diagnosis" they've had?

1771. Is there a house that gave you chills just looking at it—what made it feel spooky?

1772. Imagine hearing music instead of sirens—what upbeat tune or sound would you choose?

1773. What's one thing you're totally into, even if your friends don't share your excitement?

1774. What would your fitness wish list look like if you had someone guiding you every step?

1775. If you made a refreshing juice with your favorite fruits, what name would go on the bottle?

1776. What empowering or playful song would open your personal show?

1777. Who or what did you decorate your walls with when you were younger—pop stars, role models, or something else?

1778. Do you resist the urge to pop that pesky spot—or give in with satisfaction?

1779. Do you think Amelia Earhart's story is one of tragedy, mystery, or something else entirely?

1780. Would your look today be playful, glamorous, grumpy, or all three at once?

1781. Could you ever pull off those goofy sound effects growing up? Did you try?

1782. Do soft whispers or hair brushing videos give you those magical shivers?

1783. Think fast! What creatures come to mind when you think of the letter R?

1784. Is there a space, real or imagined, that always soothes or uplifts you?

1785. Which sci-fi invention do you secretly wish was real to make life smoother or more fun?

1786. What empowering or feel-good song would carry you through an entire week?

1787. What's something small or big you recently apologized for—and did it feel like the right move?

1788. Ever known someone named after a movie star or musician? What's their story?

1789. Is there a family recipe your mom made better than anyone else in the world?

1790. When's the last time you joined in a silly, stress-releasing pillow war?

1791. Running flat out, do you feel like a breeze, a dancer, or a flash of lightning?

1792. What playful or purposeful motto would capture the heart of a company like Google?

1793. Do you believe there should be more compassion in end-of-life decisions, and what would that look like?

1794. If you were penning a thriller, what subtle yet brilliant method would your female lead use to solve or commit a crime?

1795. What emotion or secret do you think lies behind the Mona Lisa's quiet smile?

1796. Would you be willing to trust fate and let a map decide where you go next?

1797. Which series is your guilty pleasure that you'd rather watch solo with a cozy blanket?

1798. Is there a dishwasher-loading method you believe in—and does anyone else in your house get it wrong?

1799. What's your go-to way to stop the tears when slicing onions for dinner?

1800. How would your organizing or planning habits change if sticky notes didn't exist?

1801. How did it feel the last time someone close to you said they were let down by your actions?

1802. What exclusive location would you love to explore if you had it all to yourself?

1803. Is there something you wouldn't compromise on, not even for a fortune?

1804. If your heart changed its mind right before something big, who would you turn to for support?

1805. Which game-day routine do you secretly love hearing about from your friends?

1806. Is it fair for someone to keep something valuable they found, or should they share?

1807. What's something life had to teach you the tough way?

1808. How does your current life compare to how your mom or dad lived when they were your age?

1809. What cheeky name would you love to see on a driving school billboard?

1810. What's one word that says everything you'd want people to know about you today?

1811. Have you ever shared a 'secret' you thought was yours alone, and everyone else already knew it?

1812. What's the quirkiest or most surprising museum exhibit you've ever seen or heard about?

1813. Which movie had background music so eerie it made your skin crawl?

1814. If you could style a dream costume for a mystery singer, what would be its theme or shape?

1815. When was the last time something totally unexpected turned your day upside down?

1816. When you choose a number quickly between one and ten, which one pops up for you?

1817. How do you feel about cars wearing lashes — cute, cringy, or creative?

1818. What does the idea of 'life begins at forty' mean to you personally?

1819. Was there a time you let something go because it just wasn't working out?

1820. What makes you pick up the phone for a call instead of sending a quick message?

1821. If you could reimagine the Friends characters with names that reflect strong or fun female vibes, what would you go with?

1822. Which big animal would make the cutest tiny version you'd love to carry in your purse?

1823. Have you ever had a tick scare while out in nature? What advice would you give another woman?

1824. What "magical" flavor do you think makes Coke so irresistible on a hot day?

1825. Have you ever met a woman with an elegant name that just keeps going?

1826. Which song used to feel empowering or nostalgic until it showed up in an annoying ad?

1827. What style or behavior did the popular girls have when you were a teen?

1828. Do your personal dreams evolve as you reach milestones? What new ones are you adding?

1829. What sentimental items would you want passed down to the next generation?

1830. What heartfelt wish of yours became reality—and how did that feel?

1831. Where would your dream second honeymoon take place—and who would plan it better, you or your partner?

1832. What's a detail about you that only close friends know, but feels core to who you are?

1833. If your emotions were stacked like dolls, which one would you feel safest showing?

1834. What animals make your heart melt instantly whenever you see them?

1835. Do you sing to your heart's content when your song comes on, or just hum quietly?

1836. Is there a show everyone talks about but you secretly find boring?

1837. In a moment of fear, what everyday item would you grab to feel safer?

1838. What whimsical mix of instruments would reflect your vibe—and what name would you give it?

1839. What's one mistake you'd tell other women to avoid based on your own story?

1840. What's one road sign that made you stop and laugh—or feel totally lost?

1841. As a child, did you ever imagine a secret friend? What would she be named if she returned today?

1842. What's a gem—big or small—you've uncovered lately that you can't stop recommending to your girlfriends?

1843. Who was the last person to shake your calm or disrupt your day, and how did you handle it?

1844. Imagine being allergic to something you love. Which allergy would be the hardest for you emotionally?

1845. How would you show yourself love if you had to celebrate your next birthday by yourself?

1846. What cute or quirky animal would you add to the farm song—and what sound would it make?

1847. What stylish or playful colors could make crosswalks safer and more beautiful?

1848. Is there anything you've always known isn't "you" and would never end up in your possession?

1849. Looking back at your living history, where have you felt most rooted, and how many places have you lived?

1850. Which movie do you wish had stayed untouched because the remake disappointed you?

1851. If everything turned to gray except one shade, which color would you keep to brighten your world?

1852. What was the last reason you left your workday early—planned or unplanned?

1853. Who in your circle still prints emails and asks you to "fix the internet"?

1854. Is there a sound that always makes your heart ache, no matter when you hear it?

1855. If the sky could be more beautiful in another color, what would you want it to be?

1856. What's the one thing you think The Thinker is pondering—and is it serious or silly?

1857. What image lives on your screen right now—and how often do you refresh it for inspiration?

1858. What makes your community or neighborhood feel like the right fit for you?

1859. Are you the "catch and release" type when a bug flies in—or do you go full ninja?

1860. If you had to share a space again, what's one thing your roommate absolutely couldn't do?

1861. Imagine your peaceful island retreat—what beautiful or empowering name would it have?

1862. What's your typical answer to "How are you?"—and how often does it reflect how you really feel?

1863. Was there a "thinking chair" or quiet corner in your home—and did you visit it often?

1864. What quirky kitchen item from your mom's generation have you never used yourself?

1865. What's the most recent series you watched in one go—snacks and all?

1866. What do you imagine could be hidden in the depths of the Oak Island mystery?

1867. Do you feel you click quickly with new people, or do friendships grow slowly for you?

1868. What odd or luxurious thing have you seen for sale that made you do a double-take?

1869. What was the last time a battery let you down during a moment that really mattered?

1870. What's a recent moment that made you quietly shake your head in disbelief?

1871. What world event would you undo or change to create a better future for the next generation?

1872. Which old fitness fashion do you never want to see return—unitards, neon spandex, or something else?

1873. Which colors express your spirit when you're feeling your most honest and confident?

1874. What fun or fabulous names would you give to a clowder of cats all your own?

1875. What's the kind of luxury item you'd expect to see in a billionaire's private showroom?

1876. Have you ever been on the receiving end of a wedgie? Tell me the story if you're willing.

1877. Are you someone who reflects first, or do strong instincts lead the way when things happen?

1878. What movie do you think would totally change tone if the title was about dancing instead of danger?

1879. What's your plan if you're alone in a car during a snowstorm with no help in sight?

1880. Who might be brilliant but painfully boring as dinner guests—and why?

1881. Imagine you couldn't tell a lie for a whole day—who would you quietly avoid seeing?

1882. If you could invent a fun pasta shape, what would you name it and serve it with?

1883. When was the last time you realized you were mistaken, and how did you handle it?

1884. How do you think our world will grow by the time our grandchildren are grown?

1885. Imagine a building shaped like a cupcake or purse—what oversized object would you pick?

1886. Which nostalgic theme song from your favorite show always brings a smile?

1887. How do you typically act when you've had enough and your patience runs out?

1888. Which vintage or forgotten job sounds fun or fascinating to try just once?

1889. Imagine lugging a purse and coffee up 100 floors daily—what's your game plan?

1890. Imagine having a cute fox or fluffy cat tail—what would you pick and why?

1891. What charming or creative name would you give a clownfish if it were your pet?

1892. How would having a camera in your personal space at school affect your comfort?

1893. When has a smart device helped you most, and when has it made life harder?

1894. Which female relative do you confide in most, and what makes that bond special?

1895. What part of being under the weather makes you want to curl up and cry?

1896. If your life had a soundtrack, what kind of music would win you an award?

1897. What's a rom-com or drama that was terrible but still won your heart?

1898. What kind of heartbreak lingers no matter how long it's been?

1899. What everyday moment would you turn into a song lyric for kids?

1900. In two decades, where do you hope to be calling home, and what draws you there?

1901. Which artificial fruit flavor always lets you down when compared to the real fruit?

1902. What's your easiest go-to method for eating enough fruits and veggies daily?

1903. How do you balance everyday life with your desire to be eco-conscious?

1904. Where would a hidden or poetic Banksy art piece feel powerful to you?

1905. Who have you cheered for the hardest—celebrity or loved one—and why?

1906. What do you think really happened aboard the Mary Celeste—fact, fiction, or feeling?

1907. What's your pet-inspired red-carpet name, and how glamorous (or hilarious) does it sound?

1908. What fruit do you grab first, and does it say something about your taste or wellness goals?

1909. How do you manage emotional connection when chasing big career dreams?

1910. What odd or funny road delay have you been caught in that made you laugh or sigh?

1911. Which three subjects would you keep in school to help prepare young women for the future?

1912. What cherished object holds memories that you'd be devastated to damage?

1913. How does your family handle emotional topics like death—do you speak or stay silent?

1914. What lifestyle or creative skill have you picked up from an online video?

1915. How often do you freshen up your jeans, and do you follow fashion care advice or your own?

1916. How do you balance concern for animals with advances in health and medicine?

1917. What cause, passion, or fun idea would inspire you to create your own international holiday?

1918. Do your sun sign's qualities match how you actually see yourself as a woman?

1919. What vision would you bring to life if you were gifted a large property?

1920. What once-trendy kitchen item now just takes up counter or cabinet space?

1921. Who's the fictional heartthrob or hero you would've married in a heartbeat?

1922. What do you imagine might happen to your body—or your soul—if you were sucked into a black hole?

1923. If you could design a flag for a country founded on love and equality, what would it look like?

1924. What type of work would be an absolute deal-breaker for you, no matter how well it paid?

1925. Have you ever had to run in heels or flip-flops after something flying away in the wind?

1926. Which sweet-looking animal actually has a dangerous secret?

1927. When nature calls and supplies are gone, what creative solution would you come up with?

1928. Which female or male comedian always makes you laugh, no matter your mood?

1929. What's a "never-ever" on your personal list of things to try or experience?

1930. What music would you blast as you walk into the ring, strong and confident?

1931. Do you follow any special routine when eating long noodles or pasta dishes?

1932. What's something you're known for doing well, even if your heart's not in it?

1933. How do you think facial scanning tools affect our daily privacy, especially in schools or cities?

1934. Did you ever ride a horse, even as a child or while traveling?

1935. Picture yourself as a sea captain—what's your fierce pirate name?

1936. During long waits while traveling, what's your best trick for staying calm and busy?

1937. What would be a fun twist to a fairy tale—like swapping the big bad wolf for another animal?

1938. When you share something online, what's it usually about—your life, family, or ideas?

1939. Can you believe in something even if there's no evidence yet—why or why not?

1940. What's the most creative or out-of-the-box material you'd use to build a cozy home?

1941. When were you the coldest you've ever been, and how did you cope with it?

1942. Which friend of yours eats snacks in a totally unexpected or annoying way?

1943. What show would you struggle to watch again and again without getting bored?

1944. Do people assume certain things about you because of your background or culture?

1945. When you choose earphones, do you focus more on style, comfort, or how they sound?

1946. Have you ever rushed out during a fire alarm, and what were your first thoughts?

1947. What childhood place holds the most meaning for you, and have you returned since?

1948. If you could recycle something unexpected—maybe beauty or household items—what would it be?

1949. What heartfelt community effort would you love to lead in your neighborhood?

1950. Is there a playful or expressive word you've used that you'd love to see made real?

1951. Have you experienced a situation where keeping it simple brought more peace or clarity?

1952. Is there a historical woman or figure you'd love to meet for inspiration or wisdom?

1953. What fabulous or fierce boots would show off your style if you were a storybook hero?

1954. Have you ever tossed something special by mistake and had to go get it back?

1955. What little personal habit makes you unique or "odd" in a fun way?

1956. What non-digital part of past life do you think women had a harder time doing without?

1957. If your height were a fun comparison—like a famous statue or celeb—what would it be?

1958. Has someone around you had a win or special moment this week?

1959. Who do you think has fans that cross the line from admiration to obsession?

1960. Do you tend to choose the same place to sit with friends? What does that space give you emotionally or practically?

1961. If you could safely test a boundary or rule, which one tempts you most and why?

1962. Was there a moment when you caught yourself singing a musical number while multitasking? What was it?

1963. When do you feel most grounded and recharged by nature? Is it walking, gardening, or something else?

1964. Are there street snacks that make you cringe when others eat them in public? What are they?

1965. If you could lead a brand, how would you design its look to feel vibrant, expressive, or bold?

1966. When was the last time you sidestepped a commitment, and what excuse did you use?

1967. If someone around you passed out, would you feel confident helping them? Why or why not?

1968. What emotion or theme keeps showing up in your mind today?

1969. If you could decorate your space with a famous artwork that uplifts you, what would you choose?

1970. Which TV finale left you asking, "That's it?"—and why did it feel so off?

1971. If you could shine as a one-name superstar, what name would you pick and why?

1972. Which upcoming medical or tech breakthrough do you think could change lives, especially for women or families?

1973. What female performer or changemaker do you think should be permanently celebrated?

1974. Have you ever struggled to say sorry even when your heart wanted to? Why do you think that is?

1975. Was there a sunset that made you stop and breathe deeply? Where were you and what did it mean to you?

1976. What's one spending habit you'd like to let go of to feel more financially free?

1977. If you were a treasured object, maybe a candle, book, or keepsake—what would you be?

1978. Which cultural custom, story, or site do you hope your children's children will still know about?

1979. When's the last time you got totally caught up in a task, craft, or emotion and forgot about the time?

1980. What patterns in mothering or caregiving do you think can hold children back emotionally?

1981. What sweet and catchy name would you dream up for a store-brand version of Pop-Tarts?

1982. In the past hour, did you say or think something you wish you could take back or soften?

1983. Picture this: Tom Hanks and Ozzy ring your bell. What strange emergency brought them to your doorstep?

1984. When do you rely on your head for quick math, and when do you pull out your phone or calculator?

1985. What are your thoughts on arranged marriages—especially how they affect women's autonomy and voice?

1986. Could you ever imagine eating something like that just to survive—and how would you cope afterward?

1987. Was there a style, book, or belief you loved as a teen that no longer fits who you are now?

1988. How do you handle food service issues—do you return meals or quietly accept them to avoid discomfort?

1989. What playful or soft name would you invent for a product that's basically the opposite of ultra-hold glue?

1990. If you ruled a sweet and whimsical land, what kind of treat would hang from your trees—cotton candy leaves or chocolate bark?

1991. What's the longest journey you've taken away from home, and how did it change you?

1992. When you want to feel centered or reflective, do you ever turn to classical music—and whose work speaks to you?

1993. What futuristic device could replace your smartphone—and what would you want it to do?

1994. How might a classroom pet help children feel calm, connected, or more curious about animals?

1995. Is there a moment or emotion you'd love to keep in a jar for when you need comfort or strength?

1996. Was there a time something you enjoyed became overwhelming or even stressful because there was too much of it?

1997. What's the oddest thing you've ever seen someone move on a vehicle— did it make you laugh or worry?

1998. If one color vanished from the rainbow, which one would you let go—and what would you miss about it?

1999. What do you make of people who wear sunglasses indoors—do they seem mysterious, cool, or trying too hard?

2000. Can you remember wearing something for school or work that made you feel out of place or especially confident?

2001. What food did you try after mint that totally surprised you—in a bad way?

2002. What skill would you love to master and be recognized for across the world?

2003. Which app do you use most and why does it feel like a daily go-to?

2004. Which woman or man do you think made the world better with their heart and actions?

2005. Which type of hat makes you feel stylish or comfortable, and why?

2006. What playful or poetic name would you give your very own racehorse?

2007. What confusing phrase could you say that would sound clever but make no sense?

2008. What's your dream car for comfort, beauty, or practicality?

2009. What magical or meaningful ingredient would make your pie unforgettable?

2010. Which person—actor or unexpected choice—would you love to see redefine Bond?

2011. Imagine a whimsical or powerful alien. What would you name it?

2012. What's one thing people often get wrong about you at first glance?

2013. What's your go-to way to enjoy a treat like an Oreo? Is it the same every time?

2014. What show would make you giddy to watch live in a studio setting?

2015. Have you had any meaningful or unexpected conversations while traveling by bus?

2016. If you could create a fun or elegant Jell-O flavor, what would you choose?

2017. Is there something you've chosen not to mention because you knew it before they told you?

2018. What's the book that lives in your heart and deserves to be written one day?

2019. Do your intuitions usually ring true, or do you second-guess them?

2020. What habit of yours would your friends jokingly say is a bit mad?

2021. Whose numbers live rent-free in your head even in this digital age?

2022. What's one thing you admit to being a bit particular—or even proud—about?

2023. Have you ever asked for directions and ended up with a great little story?

2024. What's one thing people think about your country or women from your country that isn't accurate?

2025. If you had wings for a day, what iconic landmark would you fly from?

2026. What moment of calm, connection, or creativity do you wish you could enjoy every day?

2027. Do you enjoy brain teasers? Which one left you saying "Wow!" after you figured it out?

2028. What's your ultimate wardrobe cringe? Something you'd refuse to wear even on a dare?

2029. Imagine you had to pick a piercing to express your style—what would you go for?

2030. What part of your pet's daily routine would you most enjoy experiencing firsthand?

2031. Have you ever watched a commercial and thought, "Who came up with that idea?"

2032. Have you ever caught yourself spiraling over something minor? What was going on?

2033. Which female artists from the 2000s made your playlists back then—and maybe still do?

2034. What dream keeps pulling you forward, even during tough seasons?

2035. If you had to wear an organ outside your body (like a necklace or accessory), which would you choose and how would you style it?

2036. Is there a theater show you've dreamed of watching live, maybe with a friend or solo?

2037. If you could safely tweak one feature for yourself, would you consider it?

2038. What little everyday frustration do you know is minor—but still gets to you?

2039. Have you taken any brave steps lately that surprised even you?

2040. Is there a kitchen from a show that you'd love to turn into your dream space—warm, cozy, or stylish?

2041. Which tree feels like your energy—peaceful like a cherry blossom or strong like an oak?

2042. What's one moment when you surprised yourself with your strength or bravery?

2043. Have you ever noticed a little mark on you that feels kind of special?

2044. What's the oddest food craving you or someone you know had during pregnancy?

2045. If you were the heartbeat of a band, which group's rhythm would you love to guide?

2046. What's a responsibility you tend to put off until the last minute?

2047. Is there a magical or sci-fi language you'd love to be fluent in just for fun or fandom?

2048. Is there a product or concept that you wish had your name on it?

2049. What fragrance or comforting scent would leave a hole if it disappeared from your life?

2050. What celebrity or historical figure seems to live or think in a way totally unlike you?

2051. Have you ever been mistaken for older or younger? What was the situation?

2052. What sport do you admire for the intense discipline it requires?

2053. What sweet or clever name would you choose for a bunny like Peter Rabbit?

2054. What's on your fridge right now that makes you smile or helps you stay organized?

2055. What name would you give to the first car that carried you through life's little adventures?

2056. Is there a type of promotional email you keep deleting that just won't go away?

2057. Where did you last escape to with family, and what memory do you treasure from it?

2058. What career path inspires you from afar, even if it's totally outside your skill set?

2059. Imagine launching your show—who would be your dream guest to start strong with heart or depth?

2060. If your doorbell could sing a tune that lifts your mood, what song or sound would it play?

2061. Is there something you said or didn't say today that you've been thinking about since?

2062. What little habit or behavior do you secretly find hard to ignore, even when you try?

2063. If you could dress up as any female character from a book, who would you choose and what would you wear?

2064. If your echo could carry one message to the world, what would you say out loud?

2065. Do you prefer to handle little home fixes yourself, like lightbulbs, or ask for help—and why?

2066. What British cultural trait stands out most to you when compared to North American life?

2067. If you were the first person to meet an alien, what would you want them to know about humanity?

2068. If you could create a sound for a reversing vehicle that's both helpful and non-annoying, what would it be?

2069. Imagine you turn into a magical or graceful creature each night—what form do you take and what's your mission?

2070. What trend or phase were you caught up in recently that you've quietly left behind?

2071. What's that one item in your fridge you keep meaning to use but just... don't?

2072. What tends to test your patience the most, and how do you usually handle it?

2073. What modern song do you think will be played at future reunions or weddings?

2074. What fictional death broke your heart—and how would you have given her a different ending?

2075. Have you ever talked your way into a better price or deal, and how did that make you feel?

2076. What's something that melts your willpower—even when you know better?

2077. What traditions do you look forward to most on national holidays, and why do they matter to you?

2078. What phrase today captures the feeling of overdoing it or not taking time to recharge?

2079. Which women in your life—past or present—deserve to be honored as your personal monument?

2080. How do you think school reading lists could better reflect students' voices and interests?

2081. Have you had to laugh off or style your way through something awkward lately?

2082. Have you found that life gives you second chances—or do you try to make your own?

2083. What's your coffeehouse favorite—and does it feel like a comfort, a treat, or a pick-me-up?

2084. If you could send a gentle, comforting dream to someone you love, what would be in it?

2085. Have you read something out loud to someone you care about lately? What was the occasion?

2086. What would you call a card company filled with warmth, humor, and beautiful design?

2087. Which sportswoman inspires you most—because of her talent, her courage, or her impact?

2088. What's a choice you make that feels right to you but seems unusual to others?

2089. What's your go-to dance-it-out song that never fails to boost your mood?

2090. What's a panini or warm sandwich filling you really love, and do you make it often?

2091. What name would you give to a firework that feels magical, elegant, and unforgettable?

2092. What would a whimsical garden gnome be hoping to reel in—sparkles, secrets, or snacks?

2093. In what situation would you let out your inner roar to be heard, respected, or seen?

2094. What do you enjoy more now that you're older—self-acceptance, confidence, or deeper friendships?

2095. When you flip a coin, do you go with your gut, or do you secretly hope for a certain side?

2096. What does a deeply satisfying life look like to you—in your heart, home, or community?

2097. What would your dream blog focus on—style, stories, or everyday reflections—and what would it be called?

2098. Which well-known woman would you love to shop with for books, outfits, or treats?

2099. What foods make watching the big game feel like a real party in your home?

2100. Which memory would you protect above all others—because of how it made you feel or what it taught you?

2101. What cozy meal makes you feel relaxed and content during a night in?

2102. What profession do you think women in the past were respected for but aren't as much today?

2103. When you're upset or overwhelmed, do you hide it behind a smile or distance?

2104. What quiet message or reminder have you been telling yourself today?

2105. If your child asked you how to tie their laces but your hands were full, how would you explain it?

2106. What's the most meaningful or stylish thing you'd want at the top of your tree?

2107. When does something go from outdated to charmingly vintage in your world?

2108. How do you soothe your nerves or recharge when life feels overwhelming?

2109. Have you ever howled or screamed just to let go of some big emotions?

2110. Where were you when time seemed to crawl, and how did you keep yourself occupied?

2111. What emotion or memory fills your heart more than anything else?

2112. Which letter would you sacrifice from your keyboard if you had to? Would it affect you much?

2113. Which health appointment do you find the most uncomfortable or nerve-wracking?

2114. What person or act recently made you clap with joy, pride, or excitement?

2115. What's a meaningful or fun way you've used coins besides spending them?

2116. Do you enjoy organizing by color? What does that say about your style or personality?

2117. What's a strange item you've heard of being shoplifted that made you laugh or gasp?

2118. If you could spend a day as a man, what would you explore or try out just for that experience?

2119. What catchy stage name would you make by mixing your favorite actress and singer?

2120. Which school subject felt like your weakness, and how did you navigate that feeling?

2121. What's something you hope people never ask, because the answer is too personal?

2122. Was there a waterfall you visited that made you pause and feel in awe?

2123. What antique baby name feels too dusty or stiff to ever sound sweet again?

2124. Have you ever peeked under the bed to feel safe before sleeping? What were you worried about?

2125. Which tiny animal makes your heart go "aww" the moment you see it?

2126. What outfit choice makes you cringe every time you see it?

2127. If your car had a horn that sounded silly, what would you want it to play?

2128. Do you remember the birthday cake that stole the show—and how old were you then?

2129. Which celebrity do you think is quiet or ordinary when they're not on stage or screen?

2130. What outfit made you feel completely empowered, like you could turn every head in the room?

2131. Which holiday film gives you that warm, nostalgic feeling every single December?

2132. What's the task today that you feel really good about accomplishing once it's done?

2133. If you had fierce karate strength for one fun moment, what would you break just for the thrill?

2134. What musical instrument do you admire most for its sound and style?

2135. When did someone or something last make you question your strength, even briefly?

2136. Have you ever bitten into something that gave you more than just a flavor—like a dentist visit?

2137. Where in the world do you think a childhood would feel like a magical adventure?

2138. Which common word mix-up never fails to make you roll your eyes or giggle inside?

2139. What part of your body would you love to take a break from once in a while?

2140. Would you ever consider making a physical sacrifice to protect or provide for someone you love?

2141. What kind of product or cause fits your values enough for you to represent it publicly?

2142. What's something people from your hometown always mention when they introduce it?

2143. What would you name a charming, fun boy band with a mix of heartthrobs and talent?

2144. When does a woman truly feel ready—heart, mind, and soul—for a lifelong partnership?

2145. Have you ever gotten fully ready for something, only to realize it wasn't even happening that day?

2146. Which beloved film have you skipped that everyone else seems obsessed with?

2147. What do you think your pet would call you if they could talk?

2148. What do we currently believe that you think future generations will disprove?

2149. What situations make you want to offer your seat to another passenger?

2150. Can you describe a moment that left you stunned or wide-eyed with wonder?

2151. Do you have a fun or specific way you enjoy eating a treat like Twizzlers?

2152. If you could share a private note with the universe, what would you write?

2153. What joyful or silly move would you add to make that song even better?

2154. What memory comes to mind when you think of the last time you had your favorite dish?

2155. If your life were a series, who would be your loyal companion—human, pet, or otherwise?

2156. What does a peaceful, joy-filled Sunday look like in your world?

2157. Do you think some things are best not asked because the answers might be painful or too personal?

2158. What's one surprising stat that made you pause or rethink something?

2159. Have you learned a lesson from assuming something about someone before really knowing them?

2160. Is there a place where you can't help but laugh when someone finds it?

2161. If you could express something meaningful through sculpture, what would you create for your town square?

2162. Have you ever sensed something would go wrong based on a feeling or superstition?

2163. What does your astrological element say about your inner self or emotions?

2164. What movie twist did someone give away before you got to watch it?

2165. What's something thoughtful or comforting you do when a friend is feeling down?

2166. What heartfelt or empowering lessons did your mom give you that you carry with you?

2167. If someone had to feed you for a while, what food would you kindly say "no thanks" to?

2168. What funny or soft word do you use when something hurts, but you're not going to curse?

2169. What woman do you admire for being quietly strong and never needing attention?

2170. If you could turn into any three things to explore or protect, what would you become?

2171. Which group games or silly playground routines made you laugh the most as a girl?

2172. What shoreline or beach felt magical to you—because of the water, the light, or who you were with?

2173. What do you admire about Switzerland's culture, scenery, or quiet elegance?

2174. What do you think about fairness and body positivity when it comes to airplane weight policies?

2175. Which fictional villain has stuck with you, whether because they were terrifying or strangely fascinating?

2176. What social expectations do women seem to follow even when no one says them out loud?

2177. If you danced in the rain and it tasted sweet, what flavor would bring you joy?

2178. What's one thing you wish existed to help balance all the things you manage?

2179. Have you bought something online or in-store that just didn't feel right, so you returned it?

2180. If you close your eyes to relax, what do you visualize—memories, dreams, or calming images?

2181. If you had the power to redesign the emotional colors of temperature, what would hot and cold be?

2182. When someone calls themselves "outdoorsy," what kind of activities or energy do you picture?

2183. Was your first coffee moment with friends, family, or during a study marathon?

2184. What's the funniest "mom moment" where you found something in the wrong place and couldn't believe it?

2185. Imagine packing for eternity—what three sentimental or meaningful things would go with you?

2186. Have you ever promised something and later felt guilty for not keeping your word?

2187. Think of a cozy or artistic name for your picture-framing boutique—what would it be?

2188. What small or big thing recently upset you, and how did you process that emotion?

2189. When you set boundaries or say no, how do you deal with the guilt or discomfort that may follow?

2190. What's a moment that made you cringe recently, whether on screen or in real life?

2191. Would you take a leap into the past or future if the science was almost safe—but not quite?

2192. What was your most memorable childhood accident, and who comforted you afterward?

2193. How do you feel about the idea that everyone gets a short burst of attention or recognition in their lifetime?

2194. What does a meaningful Christmas look like for you—emotionally, spiritually, or practically?

2195. Can you remember your first childhood crush and what made that person special in your eyes?

2196. Is there a musical icon—past or present—you wish you had the chance to see live?

2197. If snow were magical and colorful, what three dreamy hues would make winter feel enchanting to you?

2198. Which sweet childhood song would make a surprisingly awesome headbanging version?

2199. Where in the world makes you feel calm, alive, and totally at peace with yourself?

2200. Can you recall a spontaneous or silly moment when you jumped into water without changing?

2201. Picture hearing a major historical event while doing something totally normal—where would that be for you?

2202. Ever tried saying that funny woodchuck rhyme in one go? Try it now!

2203. Have you ever shared a belief others found quirky or strange but felt true for you?

2204. What would you do if you had an hour to be invisible, and how would it make you feel?

2205. Which zoo animal do you feel most connected to emotionally, and what draws you to it?

2206. If you could grow something that reminds you of family meals, what would it be?

2207. What wisdom have you gained from a time you overcame doubt or challenge?

2208. Have you ever bought something that looked fancy but wasn't? What made you do it?

2209. If you wanted to politely end a party, what tune would you put on that no one could take seriously?

2210. Is there a part of your appearance you've softened or hidden, and what story lies behind that choice?

2211. Have you ever heard a name that made you think, "That poor child"?

2212. What's your favorite way to pass the time when you're in line with friends or family?

2213. If life required you to hand over all decision-making, who would you choose, heart-first?

2214. Was there a moment at a recent wedding that felt magical, messy, or unexpected?

2215. What's something you love watching but would never sign up to do yourself?

2216. Who do you trust to back you up in a moment of trouble, even just for fun?

2217. What book felt like it spoke directly to you and should be shared with other women?

2218. Have you ever followed a hope or dream that felt magical, even if it didn't lead where expected?

2219. What film do you turn to when you need to feel deeply and maybe shed a few tears?

2220. Which Ninja Turtle's personality reminds you most of yourself?

2221. What's your first safety instinct if you're suddenly in the middle of a storm?

2222. Would any amount of money make you part with a pet that's like family to you?

2223. If you could get a futuristic body part, which one would help you most in daily life?

2224. You escape by leaping—what kind of calm or comfort would you want to find when you land?

2225. Where do you love to sit when you want to fully escape into a film?

2226. Was there ever a time you bent the rules on purpose, and what did you learn?

2227. What chocolate makes you feel a little spoiled or nostalgic every time you have it?

2228. If your smell was super-sensitive for one day, where would you absolutely not want to be?

2229. Is there a belief disguised as science that you find especially frustrating?

2230. Which woman's strength or kindness has deeply inspired you?

2231. If the Ninja Turtles had kids and careers, how would their adventures change?

2232. Was your last stapling moment about organizing or a creative fix?

2233. If you could teach one subject that speaks to your heart, what would it be?

2234. Is there a moment you look back on and wish you'd been braver or more spontaneous?

2235. What's the strangest or most memorable restaurant décor you've come across?

2236. What's your dream pair of glasses that makes you feel confident and stylish?

2237. What "bad mix" in life makes you say, "This isn't going to end well"?

2238. When your email gets out of control, how do you choose what needs your attention?

2239. Is there a kind of daring bike move you think takes the most guts and flair?

2240. What's a funny or charming way someone's described being tipsy that made you laugh?

2241. What cozy or stylish couch from a film or show would you love to spend a girls' night on?

2242. If you could lighten the mood at your funeral with a song, which one would you choose?

2243. If life gave you one more dance, who would you hold close for that moment?

2244. How do you balance savoring success with planning your next goal?

2245. Imagine shrinking a little each time you grabbed your phone—how short would you be tonight?

2246. What's your favorite backup seasoning trick when the usual spices are gone?

2247. Who's sweet but just not your style guide when it comes to clothes?

2248. Which meme do you send to your bestie that never fails to hit the spot?

2249. How do you approach a conversation about something you broke that wasn't yours?

2250. What's something you'd love to multiply in your daily life—emotionally, spiritually, or practically?

2251. What's one cozy or festive moment around food that you always carry with you?

2252. Are there expressions where you're from that feel like a warm hug or a family joke?

2253. What's the cleverest place you've hidden something sweet just for yourself?

2254. When meeting someone new, which two heartfelt or fun questions help you truly connect?

2255. What's your take on people buying pieces of history—do you think it helps or harms future generations?

2256. When do you feel most surrounded by love, care, and belonging—and who gives you that feeling?

2257. Who makes up your support circle in everyday life, and what does each one bring into your world?

2258. Do you listen to your gut or your curiosity when someone tries to guide your attention?

2259. What insect would instantly send you running for the hills?

2260. Where would you feel safe, seen, and excited to go on a first date?

2261. Which film would have felt more powerful or heartfelt with another actress playing the main role?

2262. What moment, person, or memory can instantly warm your heart and bring a smile to your face?

2263. Is there a moment you saw someone older learn the hard way that age doesn't equal wisdom?

2264. If you stumbled on a bear in the woods, what would your first thought and next step be?

2265. Can you remember a time when everything was so loud you could barely think?

2266. How would you calm down something feisty and small that's determined to stop you?

2267. Was there a childhood hiding spot that made you feel sneaky, safe, or both?

2268. Is there something your parents did that you've decided to leave out of your own story?

2269. Can you describe the scent of nature or open air in a way that brings peace to you?

2270. How do you feel emotionally when you hear about trophy hunting of animals like lions or elephants?

2271. What heels, flats, or magical shoes from a movie do you secretly wish were yours?

2272. Have you ever kept something from a friend longer than you meant to, and how did that feel?

2273. Do you have a "polite" or silly way to talk about letting one slip?

2274. What would you gently transform about yourself in a blink, if you had the power?

2275. What type of dance would let you shine and show your joy on stage?

2276. Have you ever started something that drained you more than it helped?

2277. If you could only hop, what chore or errand would you dread the most?

2278. Which place should let you stay in the car while you pick something up or drop something off?

2279. When was the last time laughter completely took over your body in the best (or most embarrassing) way?

2280. How should we deal with people who don't take responsibility for cleaning up after their pets?

2281. You're locked out—what's in your purse or nearby that you'd try using to open the door?

2282. What are some assumptions people make about Australians, especially Aussie women?

2283. Where do you keep your most private or precious papers, and how does that spot make you feel safe?

2284. How do you and others share chores at home in a way that feels balanced and respectful?

2285. What's special about the mug you love most—does it remind you of someone or something?

2286. If you could be a pampered pet for a day, who would take care of you—and how?

2287. Have you ever found yourself low on gas with no station in sight? How did it feel?

2288. What's something that made you blush in the best or most awkward way lately?

2289. Is there a movie moment that always gets you teary or moved, no matter how familiar it is?

2290. Think of a storybook elf—how would you describe her spirit, look, and purpose?

2291. Can you think of two quirky things that oddly complement each other, like glitter and grit?

2292. How do you talk about your music vibe—do you describe it, or let a playlist do the talking?

2293. Was there a moment in school when you said or did something to fit in, even if it hurt someone else?

2294. What sweet or strong name would you give a new magical reindeer on Santa's sleigh?

2295. Which English word feels most beautiful to you—whether in how it sounds or what it means?

2296. Have you ever dropped something special into the toilet? What did you do next?

2297. If you had a magic candy lab, what fun or elegant treat would you create?

2298. What kind of weather do you love most for slowing down or feeling energized?

2299. What toast color feels just right for your favorite breakfast bite?

2300. If you got paid a dollar for every time someone interrupted you, what would your bank account look like?

2301. If space travel was safe and free, would you go—and what would you hope to see?

2302. Is there a smell that wraps you in comfort or makes you feel deeply content?

2303. If your name came from a powerful goddess or magical place, what would its meaning be?

2304. What's one thing you love that others might not expect you to admit?

2305. Which dog looks like it walked out of a fashion show and a cartoon at the same time?

2306. What gadget would make your multitasking life easier without needing your hands?

2307. What business would you love to lead that feels both fulfilling and meaningful?

2308. Is there a special place in your home for something that reminds you of love or family?

2309. Have you ever used something totally unexpected while baking or cooking in a pinch?

2310. What drama, debate, or reality TV moment had you yelling from the couch?

2311. What unexpected item would you use in the kitchen to open a bottle in a pinch?

2312. What dish do you think cheese would actually make worse, not better?

2313. If you could give the world a gift from your travels, what cultural or natural wonder would it be?

2314. Imagine a cozy holiday bake—what sweet details would you decorate your gingerbread girl with?

2315. What sport would feel empowering to play professionally, and why does it inspire you?

2316. What's one thing you bought on a "treat yourself" moment that you kind of regret (or love)?

2317. What would your ideal daily life look like if you never had to work again?

2318. Who would make you giggle more than help when you're stuck on a crossword?

2319. What's the last item you mended or crafted by hand, even if it was a small fix?

2320. Is there a candy in the box you try to avoid, but end up eating anyway?

2321. Have you ever done the classic "key under the mat" trick—and was it safe?

2322. Is there a popular phrase or trend that feels forced or meaningless to you?

2323. Is there a playful or nostalgic way you like to eat a crème egg that feels a bit like self-care?

2324. What's your go-to way of being present and supportive when a loved one is spiraling?

2325. What sweet or crunchy toppings feel like the perfect indulgence on your frozen treat?

2326. What's the most relatable way you've ever heard someone describe pre-performance jitters?

2327. What does your heart dream of when it's free to wander at night?

2328. Is there someone in your world who you love so deeply you'd go to any length to keep them safe?

2329. What product or trend makes everyday life smoother or more joyful for you?

2330. What new name could still capture the magic and emotion of the Star Wars universe?

2331. Is there an aroma that makes you feel like you're walking into your childhood kitchen?

2332. How do you think public respect impacts the emotional and moral choices of women in politics?

2333. What everyday routines or roles make you feel fulfilled, even if they seem ordinary from the outside?

2334. Could you find the courage to push through fear for someone you love dearly?

2335. What cute or clever name would you give to a kids' clothing line with heart?

2336. Which noisy snack do you secretly enjoy, even if it's not the most polite?

2337. What instincts kick in when you're faced with a situation that feels unsafe for others?

2338. What's your personal way of coping with a brain freeze—and does it come with a giggle or a wince?

2339. Which animal in a cage would be the last you'd volunteer to take care of—and why?

2340. Which X-Men power would give you the edge to care for others, succeed, or stand strong?

2341. Do you know how to handle a flat tire, or would you rather phone someone who does?

2342. Is there a moment when you didn't share everything—maybe to protect feelings?

2343. What magazine would you create to inspire, inform, or connect women?

2344. If you found a gentle new life form on another planet, what imaginative name would you choose?

2345. What everyday item swap would throw everyone into delightful or disastrous disarray?

2346. Does having a tidy space help you feel more in control—or do you find joy in spontaneity?

2347. What illness do you wish no woman, child, or family ever had to face again?

2348. When did you last create something just for the fun of it—like a sandcastle?

2349. If a friend had never tried mushrooms, how would you describe their feel and texture?

2350. What does a successful life feel like for you—in your heart, your home, and your future?

2351. What wisdom or story would you want to hear from your great-grandmother?

2352. What video game sport brings out your competitive or playful side the most?

2353. Has there ever been a time you felt you had to downplay or change your profession?

2354. Imagine your favorite small animal became giant—what would be fun or scary about that?

2355. Were you ever the daring one on the playground equipment—or the one reminding others to be careful?

2356. What's your escape route if a volcano erupts and lava is heading your way?

2357. What's a trend, hobby, or choice women are unfairly judged for that you actually like?

2358. What free joys—like laughter, connection, or kindness—mean the most to you?

2359. How does your body or mood shift when you really need food?

2360. What's the strangest or most surprising hiccup cure you've been told?

2361. If you could start a movement that empowers or uplifts, what would it look like?

2362. Can you do the Vulcan "live long and prosper" sign—and what message does it send to you?

2363. What creepy-crawly would be your worst nightmare to find taking over your space?

2364. How does money affect your sense of independence or security?

2365. What colors or textures from your routine would help you go unnoticed like a superhero in disguise?

2366. If you could fly for a day, where would your wings take you for a little freedom or joy?

2367. Which Disney melody brings you back every time—joy, tears, or a full-on sing-along?

2368. If socks could talk, what story would they tell about their vanishing act?

2369. Have you ever smiled or waved at someone, thinking you knew them— but didn't?

2370. Whether out of curiosity or care, when's the last time you used your finger instead of a tool?

2371. Which two fictional people do you think would make a powerful (or delightfully weird) baby?

2372. Do you think life is meant to be complex—or are there moments of true clarity?

2373. If comfort, ease, and flavor could mix in one pot, what ingredients would you choose?

2374. Was there ever a moment you said you were older or younger to avoid judgment or feel safer?

2375. What's one thing you know, in your heart, you wouldn't sacrifice even for someone you love?

2376. Do you have a favorite "roses are red" poem or one you made that makes people smile?

2377. Have you ever heard a sweet or clever version of "roses are red" that stuck with you?

2378. Which color keeps showing up in your closet? Is it about mood, vibe, or just habit?

2379. What special thing did you dream about receiving from Santa, but he always seemed to miss it?

2380. The grill's ready, but you forgot the lighter—what clever method would you try next?

2381. Which pup would get your vote in a "most adorable dog" contest—looks, sass, or sweetness?

2382. How do you stay on top of your personal tasks while juggling everything else?

2383. Imagine you're mid-errand when an earthquake begins—what steps would you take to stay safe?

2384. What shade would you love to see in a rainbow—maybe one that reflects your spirit or dreams?

2385. Which two things do you keep by your bed every night—practical or sentimental—and why?

2386. Have you ever climbed a tree just to feel a little freer or more playful?

2387. Who's the sleepover snorer that made you giggle or stay awake all night?

2388. Was it a cozy night or girls' weekend when you last played cards? What game did you play?

2389. If the characters from Clue were real, who do you think would charm their way out of trouble?

2390. If you could eat one last meal filled with love, what would be on your plate?

2391. Have you noticed how some women grow stronger or more guarded when they're in charge? Why do you think that is?

2392. What photo feels like October to you—maybe something cozy, colorful, or quietly magical?

2393. Was there ever a time you "accidentally" broke something you secretly couldn't stand?

2394. Which emotional or dramatic story could be surprisingly fun as a glittery, feel-good musical?

2395. Was there ever a moment you softened the truth with your parents to protect feelings?

2396. On a long journey, which magical character would be just too much to handle next to you?

2397. What challenges are young girls and women facing now that you think deserve more attention?

2398. Have you attended a reunion hoping to reconnect with old friends or rediscover parts of yourself?

2399. Is your hometown still where your heart lives, or have you created a new place that feels like home?

2400. When told "don't touch," do you lean into curiosity or follow the rules?

2401. When your thoughts keep spinning at bedtime, what helps you finally relax and drift off?

2402. Which jingle from your childhood still pops into your head at the oddest times?

2403. If you could be in another woman's body for a day, whose world would you explore and how would it change your view?

2404. Have you ever stuck with something for years just to get really good at it? Was it worth it?

2405. Is there a fashion color combo that makes you cringe, even if it's trendy?

2406. What's something you've gotten good at that others never expected from you?

2407. How would it feel to relax barefoot in a comfy theater seat?

2408. What's a truth that feels too wild or wonderful to fully believe?

2409. What sound brings you peace or happiness that you'd long for most?

2410. If you had to rewrite "Keep calm and carry on" with your own spin, what would it be?

2411. What creative way would you label or sort spices so they're easy to use by feel?

2412. What did you see recently that felt like a hug to your soul?

2413. Which animal would you gladly wave goodbye to if it left with the Pied Piper?

2414. What simple pleasures today might become beautiful memories in the future?

2415. Have you ever felt proud of lighting a campfire or want to learn how?

2416. What fills you up emotionally or mentally that you always wish you had more of?

2417. Which animals swapping sounds would make you giggle every time?

2418. Is there something you witnessed that you wish you could unsee?

2419. Would you gently let someone know if their outfit needed fixing in public?

2420. What age feels like the beginning of being an elder woman in society's eyes?

2421. Who in your life do you turn to for thoughtful advice or smart ideas?

2422. What dainty party food annoys you every time it shows up at a gathering?

2423. Have you ever gotten lost in a night of dancing? What music moved you most?

2424. What's a dance you've learned that made you feel joyful or free?

2425. What flavor feels deep, mysterious, and a little magical—like the color indigo?

2426. What aspects of your workday make you feel inspired or appreciated?

2427. How would you dress a scarecrow to win a style contest—fun, chic, or totally wild?

2428. Are you the "everything neatly packed a week ahead" type, or the "frantic night-before" type?

2429. What's your best way to explain memes to someone who didn't grow up online?

2430. Do you think anything in life is ever truly free—or is there always a catch?

2431. Have you recently run late for something important? What happened, and how did you handle it?

2432. What dish or treat have you been dreaming of lately?

2433. If you could meet Walt Disney, what would you want to ask him about dreams or imagination?

2434. Have you ever seen something totally unusual cooked on a barbecue? What was it?

2435. Would you survive—or thrive—if you found yourself inside your most recent video game?

2436. Would reviving extinct creatures be a gift to nature or a risk we shouldn't take?

2437. What's your favorite delivery meal that always hits the spot?

2438. Do you think people are born with a good heart and lose their way, or can someone start out cruel?

2439. When was the last time you felt like something was just too perfect to trust?

2440. Are you someone who tops up as soon as you can, or do you run it until nearly empty?

2441. What cartoons bring back good memories or still make you smile today?

2442. Are you a "cut neatly" person or do you just tear tape however it works— teeth included?

2443. What playful name would you give to the softness we carry into adulthood?

2444. What would you turn a plain shoebox into if you had one minute and a little imagination?

2445. What's your ultimate donut treat—sprinkles, jam, cream, or something else entirely?

2446. What do you do when someone offers advice that feels intrusive or unnecessary?

2447. What's a playful or meaningful word you've imagined that should be in the dictionary?

2448. What everyday item in your home do you wish could speak its mind to you?

2449. Have you ever been "volunteered" for something no one else wanted to do?

2450. What recent day trip or getaway made you feel completely alive and joyful?

2451. Should young athletes avoid risks like heading the ball to protect their health?

2452. Who do you know that stays positive no matter what—and does it inspire or irritate you?

2453. Did you ever get a punishment that felt unfair or unforgettable when you were young?

2454. Which vehicle would you love to drive just for the joy and freedom of it?

2455. Which celebrity loss made you feel a personal sense of grief, and why?

2456. What inner voice or sign do you listen to when you're unsure which path to take?

2457. What's a playful or poetic question where "ten" would fit as the answer?

2458. Which plant-eating animal would give you chills if it suddenly became a meat-eater?

2459. Which book gave you your first proud "I read it myself" moment?

2460. Which strong or inspiring woman from history would you love to be related to?

2461. When was the last time your own writing left you wondering what you'd written?

2462. What powerful or poetic name would your all-girl rock band have?

2463. What would your heart need to know first if you'd been asleep for ten years?

2464. What's a topic you've avoided Googling because it felt too unsettling or overwhelming?

2465. Do you remember a moment when your bubble gum fun turned into a sticky situation?

2466. What winter fun do you imagine Santa's reindeer enjoying—and do they finally welcome Rudolph?

2467. If your day ended in a comically tragic way involving a round item nearby, how would it go?

2468. What type of puzzle helps you feel focused, calm, or creatively inspired?

2469. Do you ever miss the simplicity (and drama) of hanging up a call with a flip phone snap?

2470. Which apps do you rely on the most throughout your day—for calm, connection, or creativity?

2471. What's the most cringeworthy moment you've experienced in recent memory?

2472. What messy or absurd truck cargo would you least want to clean up or drive past?

2473. If you could choose a bold new color for the Hulk, what would match his fierce energy best?

2474. What kind of detailed or dreamy image would make a beautiful but maddening puzzle?

2475. Have you ever accidentally locked away something you really needed—how did you get it back?

2476. Think of something you had to wait patiently for—how did it feel when it finally happened?

2477. Is there a natural remedy you keep coming back to for comfort or wellness?

2478. Was there a cereal that made mornings magical? Do you still treat yourself to it?

2479. When you were little, what dream job made your heart light up?

2480. If your inner artist woke up today, what kind of beauty or story would you bring to life?

2481. What's something even the most stylish people can't do without looking a bit awkward?

2482. How do you feel about the idea of the death penalty? What makes it right or wrong in your eyes?

2483. Picture Blofeld in a not-so-evil moment when Bond arrives—what would make it hilariously awkward?

2484. How do you personally find comfort or meaning in the question of what lies beyond death?

2485. Have you gotten a bruise recently while doing something adventurous or unexpected?

2486. Do you ever daydream about what a stranger's life might be like—what she's feeling, where she's going?

2487. If you needed a break, what excuse would you give that no one would question?

2488. If you had a trunk like an elephant, who would you playfully surprise with a water spray?

2489. Which tongue twister is your favorite to try or teach to others?

2490. How do you feel about the idea of small daily bravery—would it help you grow or wear you down?

2491. What unusual art display sticks in your mind because it was bold, strange, or emotional?

2492. What instinct would kick in if a dog started running toward you while you were out for a walk?

2493. What animal mashup would you invent—cute, wild, magical, or just weird?

2494. Can you recall the moment you felt pulled toward a role or calling that made you feel fulfilled?

2495. Which flaw in someone's personality feels especially hard for you to be around?

2496. When was a time you felt either super overdressed or underdressed—and how did you handle it?

2497. Is there a dream that keeps coming back to you—what do you feel it's trying to say?

2498. Is there a household task you secretly dread, even if it's small?

2499. What helps you feel replenished when you're running on empty—mentally or physically?

2500. Which under-the-radar show do you always recommend to your friends?

2501. What local landmarks in your hometown would be considered luxury on a Monopoly board?

2502. What two words might your coworkers or classmates say reflect who you really are?

2503. If you were a houseplant, which one reflects your style—nurturing, blooming, or grounded?

2504. What shopping experience left you thinking, "Never again"?

2505. Do you think your pet understands your tone or feelings when you talk to them?

2506. What unique club, place, or group from your younger years do you sometimes long for?

2507. What's your go-to routine or comfort when you feel overwhelmed or anxious?

2508. If your friends had to compete in a light-hearted throwing contest, who would you bet on?

2509. What childhood book or film character made you feel seen or understood?

2510. If you had to explain football to someone new, how would you make it relatable?

2511. Which restaurant do you go back to over and over again, and do you switch it up or stay loyal to one meal?

2512. Where in history would an angry hippo cause the most dramatic scene?

2513. Can you shout out three Beatles tunes in ten seconds flat?

2514. What banana treat feels like a comfort food or nostalgic memory?

2515. Have you ever bent the rules and felt guilty—or relieved?

2516. Have you caught yourself drifting off into thoughts when you were supposed to be listening?

2517. What color would you choose for a red carpet that feels elegant and empowering?

2518. What medical moment would be your worst fear to wake up during?

2519. Which colors with yellow would make a stunning outfit or home look?

2520. Have you ever had a moment where you looked in the mirror and felt different inside or out?

2521. When was the last time you did something brave, bold, or out of character—and surprised everyone?

2522. What's something that had you yawning non-stop—was it sleepiness or something else?

2523. What funny or magical sound would you want your cough to make instead?

2524. Is there a color you avoid because it washes you out or feels off?

2525. Did you have to resist touching something delicate or special in your childhood home?

2526. Who's someone whose kindness or confidence makes them truly beautiful in your eyes?

2527. Are there jobs that benefit from emotional intelligence or empathy where women thrive more?

2528. What moments in history, especially for women or families, were happening when you were born?

2529. Would you go as Princess Leia, Rey, or design your own galactic outfit?

2530. Which celebrity's voice you love but think they should stay off the screen?

2531. Do you take time to untie your shoes, or are you more of a slip-out-and-go type?

2532. What's a food name that made you pause, laugh, or Google it before eating?

2533. If you won money from a fundraiser, would your first thought be to give back or enjoy it?

2534. What's a poetic way to describe taking the scenic route?

2535. Do you practice kindness in the same way you wish to receive it?

2536. Which phrase feels the most outdated or patronizing to you?

2537. What self-care items are non-negotiables in your weekend bag?

2538. What charming or quirky find have you taken home from a garage sale?

2539. What part of who you are makes you feel beautiful or confident inside?

2540. If you could restyle the White House like a dream home, what shade would it wear?

2541. How do you handle an overly hot bite of food when you're trying to stay composed?

2542. Which emoji always makes its way into your group chats?

2543. If Lady Liberty were reimagined today, what meaningful item should she raise instead?

2544. What are two names you imagine on cheerleaders or prom kings in old movies?

2545. Have you ever had the urge to push a button just because it's shiny and red?

2546. Would you accept the no-lick donut challenge for fun?

2547. Imagine using whiskers to sense doorways—how long would yours have to be?

2548. What car says "elegant and established" without being flashy?

2549. If you could live in a different era for good, which time would you choose and why?

2550. Which name-song makes you sing along every time?

2551. Where in life do you feel quality trumps quantity?

2552. What personal trait reminds you most of your mom or grandmother?

2553. Which childhood bedroom or kitchen wall would you want stories from?

2554. Can you remember the last time you chose spontaneity over planning?

2555. Have you had to reschedule something you were excited about recently?

2556. Should kids and teens be celebrated in gaming with something like a Fortnite World Cup?

2557. What sappy song do you secretly tear up to when no one's watching?

2558. How would you tell a teammate they need a mint—without embarrassing them?

2559. What social pressure or habit do you think we should stop pretending is okay?

2560. What shape would make Earth feel more magical or surreal if it weren't a globe?

2561. What chore or task do you wish you could breeze through in seconds?

2562. Even on an outdoor adventure, what's the one fun or cozy item you'd sneak into your backpack?

2563. What multitasking moment had you wishing for a third hand—or two more?

2564. Can you remember what you thought about babies before you knew the facts?

2565. What weird or wild story have you heard that made you say, "No way"?

2566. Even with millions, what part of your life or self would you hold onto?

2567. What groups or social circles have you outgrown?

2568. Did anyone ever tell you something funny or strange you did in your sleep?

2569. What food is delicious warm but turns yucky when it's not?

2570. When was a time something big happened and you felt like everything changed?

2571. When have you gone along with something just to be polite or avoid conflict?

2572. Do you think women in the far future will have different features or abilities?

2573. Would you travel across cities (or countries!) to complete something you love collecting?

2574. Is there a company you keep choosing again and again—what makes it your favorite?

2575. If you had the chance to buy stock in any company long ago, which one would you choose?

2576. Are you the kind of person who follows a strict brushing pattern or switches it up?

2577. What's the last wish you'd make if you had just one more left?

2578. Has your journey so far felt more uphill than most people's?

2579. What would you never reuse or share with others, even if it saves money?

2580. Where were you the last time you danced like a kid again?

2581. What's the pasta you'd gladly eat forever if no other shape existed?

2582. If your vibe were a cheese, would it be rich and creamy or something with a kick?

2583. If someone watched your daily routine, which animal would they say you're most like?

2584. What game show do you dream of being on where you'd totally shine?

2585. What's the final touch that makes something truly perfect in your world?

2586. Which silly cartoon invention would actually come in handy in your real life?

2587. Is there a book that gave you clarity or comfort when you needed it?

2588. What old kids' show do you look back on and think, "That was kind of strange"?

2589. If your essence was bottled, what would your three standout qualities be?

2590. What would your dream wearable do—track emotions, clean your face, or something else?

2591. If you unplugged from social media for a week, how would it feel—liberating or lonely?

2592. Who's a woman or man who lifts your spirits just by being who they are?

2593. What kind of comment makes you instantly guard your energy?

2594. Has someone ever let you down so much that your opinion of them changed forever?

2595. What's something you fiercely protect about yourself or your life?

2596. What's a habit or chore you once promised yourself you'd avoid—but didn't?

2597. What brand do you think would turn the moon into its next showroom?

2598. What's a wellness fad you've followed that now makes you laugh?

2599. Would your dream role be worth hours on the road—or would you reconsider?

2600. What random thing from your bag or home could double as a straight edge?

2601. What tasks were always yours at home, and did you feel appreciated for doing them?

2602. What daring, yet stylish, way would you cross the Grand Canyon if you had to?

2603. What restaurant décor makes you feel welcome and comfortable?

2604. Have you ever played limbo at a party, and how did it go?

2605. When was the last time emotions got the best of you and you left a space?

2606. Is there a word you triple-check every time because you just don't trust it?

2607. Do you think some moments in life are so surprising they feel like miracles?

2608. What's your favorite way to express excitement without saying "awesome"?

2609. What kind of people leave you feeling emotionally drained or unheard?

2610. If someone described you in a single empowering line, what would that line be?

2611. What common item would seem like pure magic in a time before technology?

2612. What kind of decor or vibe in a restaurant helps you truly unwind?

2613. What's something you lost and felt super relieved to find again?

2614. If life were a mood tracker, what would your happiness reading be today?

2615. What dream are you holding onto fiercely, even if others think it's unrealistic?

2616. Did anyone ever tell you what soothed your baby self when you wouldn't sleep?

2617. Would you stop the bus for someone who's clearly giving it their all to catch up?

2618. What feels like magic now but will probably be normal in your grandchildren's time?

2619. Have you ever felt out of sync with yourself—and what pulled you back in?

2620. What cloud shape feels like a soft breath or cozy blanket in the sky?

2621. What book title would reflect your story of strength, love, and surprises?

2622. Is there a rule or regulation today that you believe limits women's choices, but might be seen as outdated in the future?

2623. What little food habit makes you feel in control or comforted—like how you spread your peanut butter?

2624. Which movie road trip scene made you want to escape for a while or feel adventurous?

2625. If two items are exactly the same, what makes you pick one brand over the other—style, message, or feeling?

2626. What's a little item that always goes missing in your home, and it drives you a little nuts?

2627. Can you recall a time when something small, like snow falling, made you feel wonder or warmth inside?

2628. Do you have any at-home exercise gear that's become more of a habit or more of a decoration?

2629. How do you balance personal choice and community health when it comes to vaccine decisions for women and families?

2630. Can you recall your last birthday wish? Did it reflect a dream, a person, or something you wanted to change?

2631. What comforting or favorite food would you crave most if you could only drink your meals for a week?

2632. What letter do you love writing, seeing, or using—and does it remind you of someone or something special?

2633. When you hear the word 'home,' is there a cozy corner, a person, or a moment you think of first?

2634. Which world leader do you think would not understand your country's people or values at all?

2635. Did you ever act or sing in front of others at school? How did you feel about your part?

2636. What trend once made you feel excited, but now just feels overdone or less unique?

2637. Would you want to be told if the world was ending tomorrow, or would you rather soak in your final hours without worry?

2638. Is there a holiday tradition that's stayed strong in your family and always brings a warm feeling?

2639. Can you remember a time you were wearing odd socks or shoes and didn't notice until later?

2640. Was there something you meant to do, but forgot, and it caused more trouble than you thought it would?

2641. What's something you would never want to advertise on your body—no matter how much money they offered?

2642. Have you ever done the 'Baby Shark' hand motions, maybe with a little one or just for fun?

2643. When did you last move your body for exercise or joy, and what kind of movement was it?

2644. If you were cast in a reality show, which one fits your personality—and would it challenge or excite you?

2645. Which song with a weekday in the lyrics speaks to you—joyful, reflective, or somewhere in between?

2646. What kind of cake do you enjoy but find hard to finish a second slice of?

2647. Was there ever a time when someone else took the blame for your actions, even if you didn't mean for it to happen?

2648. What's the strangest remedy you've heard about or tried for head lice when growing up?

2649. Do you have a go-to pizza crust that feels like the perfect base for your toppings?

2650. Picture yourself as a butterfly—what beautiful or meaningful colors would your wings be?

2651. Which silly cat clip still cracks you up when you think about it?

2652. Which languages can you say basic greetings in, and do they connect to any special memories?

2653. Have you ever seen a piece of taxidermy that was so odd or surprising you couldn't forget it?

2654. If you could only keep one pen color—blue, black, or something bold—which one reflects you best?

2655. What task in your day would be the most entertaining or frustrating to perform super slowly?

2656. What was it like the last time you couldn't speak out loud—how did you stay connected?

2657. What place in nature makes your heart feel full—maybe a meadow, a beach, or a sunrise view?

2658. When you're coloring, do you like the structure of the lines or the freedom of ignoring them?

2659. Do you tend to pick up on someone's eyes, voice, or warmth first when you meet them?

2660. Who's the person you'd invite over when you want to talk, laugh, or just feel understood?

2661. Do you remember the last handwritten note or list you made—maybe something heartfelt or routine?

2662. Have you ever playfully buried someone at the beach—head sticking out and all?

2663. What color rain would feel magical or beautiful falling from the sky just once?

2664. When you imagine aging, what concerns you most—appearance, energy, or something deeper?

2665. Which surprising celebrity do you think would make a fun or awkward James Bond?

2666. Is there a female-led or fantasy anime that resonated with you growing up or now?

2667. Which playful or creative term for money always makes you smile or reminds you of someone?

2668. Have you ever said you loved a book, show, or brand just to feel accepted or interesting?

2669. What fun or decorative idea could you make using just empty egg cartons?

2670. Have you found that personal experience makes you believe something more than stories ever could?

2671. Which popular song makes you feel confident dancing because you've memorized every part?

2672. Have you ever used a Hoppity Hop, and did it make you laugh or feel like a kid again?

2673. If you had no fear of danger, what bold experience would you want to have—solo travel, cliff diving, something wild?

2674. When you exercise, do you need a playlist, a calming voice, or nothing at all to stay present?

2675. Are there times when you expect yourself to be flawless, even if no one else does?

2676. What playful or cozy name could you give mashed potatoes to make them sound even more comforting?

2677. Have you ever answered the phone using a different voice or name—just to be funny or clever?

2678. What kind of snake creeps you out the most, and does it have to do with how it moves or looks?

2679. When you're trying to get a friend's attention in a crowd, what's your go-to move?

2680. How would you describe your parents in three words—thinking of how they make you feel or act?

2681. What did you do during your longest-ever wait in a waiting room—read, people-watch, daydream?

2682. Is there a typical thing people your age often do that you haven't tried yet?

2683. Which cake would you keep forever if all others had to go—comforting, rich, or nostalgic?

2684. What part of a job offer—culture, flexibility, values—would be a clear deal breaker for you?

2685. What was the last thing you looked at in a shop window and felt drawn to—but didn't buy?

2686. Are your eating times consistent, or do they change based on mood or schedule?

2687. What detail from your favorite park made it feel magical—was it a garden, fountain, or path?

2688. Where would your inner cat curl up for comfort—a sunlit window, a soft blanket, or hidden nook?

2689. What's a fear you carry that's tied to protecting others or yourself?

2690. What's your comfort zone when it comes to heights—where does courage turn to caution?

2691. What name would you give baby octopuses to make people smile or say "aww"?

2692. When did a small or big realization recently help you solve something or change your thinking?

2693. If your first-choice career didn't happen, what's another role that would still feel meaningful to you?

2694. What dreamy or magical image would you use to express "yeah, right" in another world?

2695. Have you ever seen your words or actions cause heartbreak, and how did you deal with that moment?

2696. What shape or trick do you use when you want your paper plane to fly far or look cool?

2697. Is there an animal noise you can imitate that always gets a reaction or makes you giggle?

2698. What's one part of life that continues to catch you off guard or feel unnatural?

2699. Would you ever bungee jump? If yes, where would feel both terrifying and beautiful to try it?

2700. What's the last unexpected moment where everything just lined up strangely or magically?

2701. Have you ever had a Monopoly match that seemed like it might never end?

2702. If you had the chance to have tea or lunch with a Beatles member, who would it be and why?

2703. Where and when did you last feel that fizzy, tickly 'pins and needles' feeling?

2704. Was there an experience you didn't say yes to that still feels like a what-if moment?

2705. What's the wildest or silliest hat you've ever seen someone wearing in public or a party?

2706. If walking made a noise each time, what sound would you love hearing under your feet?

2707. Is there a historical look—flowy dresses, corsets, or iconic hair—you'd love to revive?

2708. How do you balance being responsible with keeping a sense of playfulness or freedom?

2709. Is there a shape you associate with beauty, softness, or strength—what does it represent to you?

2710. What's a playful or surprising talent you bring out when the mood is light and fun?

2711. Which game do you think has the characters or story to become an amazing show?

2712. Would your conscience nudge you to write a note if you nicked someone's car in public?

2713. What whimsical or sweet name could describe a whole bunch of playful five-year-olds?

2714. Have you written a thank-you note lately? Who was it for, and what did you say?

2715. Have you crossed paths with someone famous, and did anything about them surprise you?

2716. What odd or funny mix of ingredients have you turned into a sandwich just to try something new?

2717. If you were creating a store display, what mood or idea would you want people to feel as they walk by?

2718. Is there a commercial you still remember vividly—maybe one that made you feel something strong?

2719. What shadows or shapes in the dark used to make your imagination run wild?

2720. Which herbal or plant-based treatments have supported your wellness and comfort?

2721. Did you ever share a playful code or ritual with close friends that felt like a fun secret?

2722. If you could customize your remote with one magical button, what would it control?

2723. In an alternate reality, what are you doing that feels totally different from your current self?

2724. If we were to rephrase 'strong as an ox' in today's world, what empowering or funny twist would you give it?

2725. Have you had a moment recently where something slipped out and you instantly wanted it back?

2726. What would fill a store designed to sell tiny annoyances—socks that slide down, pens that don't work?

2727. Have you ever known someone from Australia named Bruce or Sheila— or is that just something people say?

2728. Is there a moment in history class you still remember clearly—what made it stay with you?

2729. How did you learn how long you could go without breathing—was it playful or competitive?

2730. What's one interview question that stayed with you for how challenging or strange it was?

2731. What would go through your mind if you stumbled on an abandoned bag of money?

2732. What are a few little things that never fail to bring a smile to your face or calm your heart?

2733. Was there a bumper sticker that made you smile or think, "That's so true"?

2734. Do you remember the last time you made a snow angel—was it joyful, nostalgic, or spontaneous?

2735. Which story of transformation and perseverance lifts your spirit when you think of it?

2736. If you switch between languages in your head, when does it happen and what triggers it?

2737. What name would you give Frodo to reflect his loyalty, kindness, and quiet bravery?

2738. What memory comes to mind when you think about the last time you wore waterproof boots?

2739. Which childhood plush or soft toy would you take to a sweet, nostalgic picnic and why?

2740. Which popular Gen Z expression leaves you thinking, "What does that even mean?"

2741. Are there foods you'll still eat if they fall, or does the 'rule' go out the window?

2742. If road signs could be more emotional or realistic, what message would yours deliver?

2743. If your meal had an unpleasant surprise, how would you handle it—stay calm or walk away?

2744. Is there someone in your life whose noise fills a room before they even walk in?

2745. What sound would you love your toaster to make—something magical, silly, or soothing?

2746. Was there a moment where you felt deeply that life should be richer, fuller, or more connected?

2747. What cape color would reflect your strength, kindness, or courage if you were a heroic figure?

2748. Was there a word you recently had to look up to fully understand or use it properly?

2749. When do you think is a good time to move out and create your own space and rhythm?

2750. Have you revived any devices recently by turning them off and back on—old trick, still works?

2751. Have you ever put together a secret gathering or surprise party that lit someone up with joy?

2752. What do you hold onto with all your heart—because it's part of your truth, your hope, or your dream?

2753. How would you respond in a moment of total surprise and fear—like seeing a snake while showering?

2754. What sweet or quirky name could replace 'peanut butter' and still feel deliciously familiar?

2755. What dish would carry your name if you were known for your food and flavors?

2756. Is there a lost animal you wish still roamed the Earth—what draws you to it?

2757. What destination required the longest flight you've taken—and what did you do to stay sane onboard?

2758. Was there a game or trend you loved (or avoided) during your schoolyard days?

2759. If your house had a hidden tunnel, what magical or meaningful place would it lead to?

2760. How do you balance doing what's easy with doing what helps you grow?

2761. What better-for-you food surprised you by being even more delicious than the usual version?

2762. When a button pops and you're stuck, how do you improvise to keep it together—literally?

2763. What's something that startled you out of sleep—and how did you feel afterward?

2764. If you were rebranding the trains in today's world, what creative or stylish names would you choose?

2765. What simple or surprising card trick do you recall learning first—and what made it stick?

2766. Do you wait or wander when a website stalls—what's your attention span for tech delays?

2767. What's your favorite order when you're craving something warm, spiced, and satisfying from Indian cuisine?

2768. If you found a ring that seemed very special, how would you handle returning it?

2769. What pickled treat do you love for its bold flavor and satisfying bite?

2770. Have you ever been asked to pet-sit, and what animal did you care for?

2771. What lighthearted name would you invent for the squishy spot where your arm folds?

2772. What's your most recent or memorable faceplant moment, and did you laugh it off or blush?

2773. Which puzzling mystery from the world or history would you most want answers to?

2774. What playful or peaceful things might you mentally count when you're struggling to fall asleep?

2775. What dramatic look would you choose to wow a crowd at a glamorous party or award show?

2776. What kind of list did you write most recently—was it practical or personal?

2777. If you stumbled on buried treasure near your home, what would you secretly wish it contained?

2778. Why do you think glue doesn't dry up inside its own container?

2779. In what situation would you love to be able to switch hands and still do a task with ease?

2780. If you were invited to tea with royalty, who would you hope to be seated beside?

2781. What experiences or choices would go straight on your 'hard pass' list?

2782. What humorous or accurate name could describe a lively bunch of teens?

2783. Have you ever purchased duplicates thinking you'd use both—but didn't?

2784. What item or experience did you choose to buy when you first made your own money?

2785. If another world had living creatures, how do you picture them?

2786. What tasty picks do you go for when assembling your perfect salad plate?

2787. Do you own or love a handy gadget that's two-in-one—like a pen with a secret feature?

2788. Was there a piece of graffiti that moved you, made you laugh, or sparked a thought?

2789. Did you ever pull off a yo-yo trick that made others stop and watch?

2790. Is there something you attempted, only to discover it definitely wasn't your hidden talent?

2791. When a picture's being taken, do you have a favorite pose or natural instinct?

2792. When and what was your very first drink—and how did you feel about it?

2793. What's a surprising little fact you carry around just in case someone asks?

2794. What's one thing you did as a kid that makes you wonder how you survived it?

2795. If you had your moment of glory on a snowboard, what trick would you be known for?

2796. What setting did you last watch a sunrise in—peaceful, energizing, or emotional?

2797. Which power ballad or rock song would sound beautifully odd sung by a barbershop quartet?

2798. Have you ever stashed change in a jar and felt proud watching it grow?

2799. Have you ever kept going while quietly learning, even if you didn't feel ready yet?

2800. What's the quirkiest challenge or game you've ever read about or seen?

2801. What was your most recent daydream—and what feelings did it leave you with?

2802. Do you remember doing handstands in the water—how recently did you flip upside down?

2803. What monkey moment would bring you the most joy—climbing, swinging, or just eating fruit all day?

2804. When was the last time you had to explain yourself after doing something you shouldn't have?

2805. Did you ever raise a Tamagotchi, and did it survive more than a week?

2806. How did your parents react the first time you said something you weren't supposed to?

2807. If your journey had a villain, who—or what—would it be that challenged your growth?

2808. Do you rely on a specific start to your day, or are you more go-with-the-flow?

2809. What small comfort or community detail would tug at your heart if you had to say goodbye?

2810. Which funny or clever palindromes do you enjoy using or hearing?

2811. How do you wrestle with the concept of war—necessary evil or a tragic failure?

2812. If you had to row across the sea in a wacky way, what would you float in?

2813. If you had a trucker-style nickname, what would yours say about you?

2814. Where do you spend most of your time online—whether for info, fun, or connection?

2815. When watching or reading a mystery, do you try to guess the ending or just enjoy the ride?

2816. What moment—big or small—recently reminded you that people can be amazing?

2817. If a new Ninja Turtle joined the crew, what name would suit them best?

2818. What was the first horror flick that made you peek through your fingers?

2819. If cat clips were gone, what do you think people would watch to feel cozy or laugh?

2820. Living forever sounds amazing, but what do you think would be the biggest cost?

2821. Do you feel nostalgia when you think of school—or was it more of a survival story?

2822. What's something in your closet you keep but never wear—and why do you still have it?

2823. What pet would you never want because it's just too uneventful or hard to bond with?

2824. Is there someone in your life whose age inspires you with stories or perspective?

2825. What look or accessory feels forever stylish to you, no matter the decade?

2826. Have you ever gently ended things by shifting the focus to yourself—how was it received?

2827. When was the last time you reached for a DVD instead of streaming—and what did you watch?

2828. What part of your day would become most challenging without being able to squat or kneel?

2829. If you had a fairy godmother for a day, what single act of magic would you hope for?

2830. How did you respond when you realized the support you expected wasn't arriving?

2831. When does heat go from pleasant to unbearable for you?

2832. What were you always excited to buy with your allowance as a kid?

2833. How do you feel about making the bed—must-do ritual or occasional effort?

2834. If a superhero that size drove a car, what kind of comically bad fit would it be?

2835. If mint disappeared from toothpaste forever, what fresh or fun taste would you want instead?

2836. What setting made you feel unseen or emotionally distant even though you weren't alone?

2837. Do you remember the first movie you ever saw in a theater—and who took you?

2838. Where did you last go camping, and how did it feel to sleep under the stars?

2839. Which song would be hilariously awkward as a couple's first dance at their wedding?

2840. If you flew a balloon in the sky, what image or phrase would you proudly display?

2841. What orange-flavored snack or sip brings you the most joy?

2842. Would you be ready to help with CPR if someone needed it right now?

2843. What fresh experience recently gave you a thrill, a lesson, or a surprise?

2844. When did you take a walk that pushed your limits—how long did it last?

2845. What gathering or meeting drained your energy simply by being unbearably boring?

2846. If someone offered to take over your to-do list for 24 hours, where would they start?

2847. What prize would make you smile politely while thinking, "What am I supposed to do with this?"

2848. Is there something you've hidden that you're finally ready to confess?

2849. What smell would be so bad that even a tiny sticker of it would ruin your day?

2850. Why does telling yourself not to think something only make it louder in your brain?

2851. What little moment, plan, or break makes you feel optimistic about tomorrow?

2852. Which emoji do you scroll past every time, knowing it's just not your vibe?

2853. If you could start again in another form, what would you choose—animal, artist, explorer?

2854. Who in your family do you call, text, or visit the most—and why?

2855. If someone could cook you anything right now, what meal would feel perfect?

2856. What three qualities make you feel safe, motivated, and valued by a boss?

2857. What lesson came to you only after the second (or third) time of messing it up?

2858. What was the story behind the most expensive shoes you ever bought?

2859. If you were in a goofy chip challenge, how many Pringles would you try to stuff in?

2860. What role could Keanu Reeves play if he stepped into your world for a movie version of your story?

2861. Was there an ad that made you avoid a product altogether—even if it was good?

2862. What fate do you feel is too harsh to wish on even someone who wronged you deeply?

2863. If you designed your own underground retreat, what would be inside— practical, fun, or both?

2864. What did you do the last time you walked into a room and forgot what you came for?

2865. What food item would totally ruin your pocket and make you wish you never tried it?

2866. What's one thing you guard closely because of its value—emotional, practical, or symbolic?

2867. If you could be remembered for discovering something, what would it be and why?

2868. How do you make the hard call when dessert decisions feel like heartbreak?

2869. Where could a dream offer never persuade you to relocate—what's your hard boundary?

2870. What did today teach you that you didn't know this morning?

2871. If imagination and Lego were endless, what dream build would you bring to life?

2872. What joke from your childhood still lives in your memory, word for word?

2873. Have you crossed paths with someone named Karen who was actually the nicest person?

2874. Where do you listen to your favorite playlists—any reason you prefer that platform?

2875. When life gets scary or uncertain, who's your comfort person in crisis?

2876. If you could sum up your childhood bedroom in a single word, what would it reveal?

2877. Have you ever watched a tadpole grow legs up close—was it a school project or backyard adventure?

2878. What mix of items in your shopping basket once made the cashier raise an eyebrow?

2879. What's your biggest soft spot when it comes to splurges or indulgences?

2880. What's a story from your childhood that's both naughty and a little funny now?

2881. What's your personal boiled egg rule—firm, soft, or somewhere in between?

2882. What kind of DIY skill would you love to feel confident doing all on your own?

2883. If you had to guess who's living a double life at work or school, who's your pick?

2884. Which fashion fad are you convinced won't survive the next decade?

2885. When's the last time you were caught off guard by the weather and got soaked?

2886. Which trio of letters gets the most wear from your typing habits?

2887. Is there someone on screen that makes you think, "I probably won't like this movie"?

2888. What thought or feeling greeted you first today when you started your morning?

2889. If you could spend a day living someone else's life in your circle, who would it be—and what would you try?

2890. What cozy or fun spot would you create to escape, recharge, or be your full self?

2891. If juggling became your wild talent, what fun or risky items would you use to perform?

2892. Have you recently seen lightning light up the sky—what did you feel in that moment?

2893. In a world overrun by zombies, what object would you count on to keep you safe?

2894. What trait would you want others to think of first when they speak your name?

2895. Can you imagine a world where humans and dinosaurs lived side by side?

2896. Which types of YouTube videos do you turn to when you want to unwind, learn, or laugh?

2897. Do you remember the days of carrying music in your pocket with a cassette Walkman?

2898. What unexpected piece of news or gossip took you by surprise lately?

2899. If you had the agility of a cat, what dream or dare would you finally go after?

2900. What childhood obsession did people assume you'd drop—but it's still part of your identity today?

2901. What's your relationship with public speaking—dread, growth, or somewhere in between?

2902. If you had a peaceful rooftop moment to yourself, where would it be and what would you see?

2903. When's the last time you threw up, and what do you remember about the moment?

2904. If everything went your way, what would your most perfect day include?

2905. What creative band name could you invent using the initials of three of your best girlfriends?

2906. What's your go-to Mexican food when you're hungry for something delicious and familiar?

2907. If your body was made of Play-Doh, what fun or empowering changes would you make?

2908. What encounter left you thinking, 'That was unnecessarily rude'?

2909. What early gaming memory sticks with you—and what game started it all?

2910. If you had extra-long hair like Rapunzel, what creative styles would you try?

2911. If you reinvented the egg-and-spoon race, what would be the silliest combo to run with?

2912. Have you ever pulled something tiny out of the dryer and realized it used to fit?

2913. What experience recently made you feel disappointed or taken advantage of?

2914. Could you walk away with one kitten while the other watched you leave?

2915. What odd moment of synchronicity left you thinking, "That can't be real"?

2916. When was the last time you actually read all the terms and conditions?

2917. If someone stood out in the family, what nickname or saying could describe them playfully?

2918. Has anyone ever caught you doing something gross that made you cringe later?

2919. If you could design the most ridiculous faux rug ever, what animal would it copy?

2920. What's the tipping point when rhyming goes from clever to cringey?

2921. If your life story were on a shelf, what teaser would make someone want to read it?

2922. If you could invent a new Spice Girl identity, what would her name and vibe be?

2923. What's one vegetarian meal you love for its taste, texture, or comfort factor?

2924. Have you ever misjudged where to park and felt guilty afterward?

2925. Which illness would shake you to hear—and why?

2926. How would you balance fun and individuality when dressing your identical twins?

2927. What wild idea would you bring to life to build the ultimate roller coaster?

2928. Who's famous in your circle for their hilariously lazy cooking methods?

2929. Have you recently chosen the stairs over the elevator—and how did it feel?

2930. How closely do your words align with your true thoughts and feelings?

2931. What's the most unexpected thing you found yourself pondering in the shower lately?

2932. What would be your signature performance if you toured with a circus?

2933. Who in your family is hilariously confused by smartphones, remotes, or computers?

2934. Have you ever taken a risk that went against a posted safety guideline?

2935. If someone ran out of toilet paper, what would you strongly recommend they NOT use?

2936. What would have to happen for you to believe eating human flesh was your only option?

2937. What childhood fear did you eventually face or overcome with time?

2938. When have you taken a wild chance just for the thrill of it?

2939. What's one thing you wish people would stop stressing about so much?

2940. What creative or poetic wording would sum you up as a high-end restaurant dish?

2941. What did you discover clinging to your shoe that made you cringe—or laugh?

2942. What moment had you second-guessing yourself with a laugh or a sigh?

2943. What meaningful or practical items would you stuff into a bandana to carry over your shoulder?

2944. When you shower, do you follow the same steps every time or mix it up?

2945. What frozen artwork stood out to you as surprisingly detailed or beautiful?

2946. Is there a word you stumble over even though you know what it means?

2947. What big call did you have to make lately—and did it feel right in the end?

2948. What does your morning prep look like—and is it quick or leisurely?

2949. What are your non-negotiable 'must be peeled' foods?

2950. Would you turn in or keep a lost envelope of money—why or why not?

2951. Did something once fool you into thinking it was authentic when it wasn't?

2952. What's something you waited a long time for and ended up being glad you did?

2953. If your bathing suit slipped off in the sea, how would you handle it with grace?

2954. What book did you just read, and how many stars would you give it?

2955. What face painting design did you love the most when you were a child?

2956. What's something you did or didn't do recently that stayed on your mind?

2957. What's the most sentimental or durable thing still hanging in your closet?

2958. Which lost-and-found animal story sticks with you the most emotionally?

2959. If your mugs disappeared, what unusual thing would you pour your hot drink into?

2960. When did something small feel like too much—and what did it lead to?

2961. What was it like to be present during a solar eclipse?

2962. If you opened the fridge and saw a raccoon helping itself, how would you react?

2963. Do you remember what you last cleaned up with a broom—and why?

2964. How would you describe your mom in a single word that means the most to you?

2965. Have your go-to apps or social hangouts changed over the past year?

2966. Is there something you do in your home that's normal for you but odd to outsiders?

2967. Who got your message by mistake—and what was their reaction?

2968. Which family from books, shows, or movies would be the worst real-life relatives?

2969. What moment stands out when you felt torn between fitting in and being yourself?

2970. Where would you go or what would you do to feel safest during a tornado threat?

2971. What do you recall from your last train trip—destination, view, or mood?

2972. If you were writing a detective show, what two names would make the lead female duo unforgettable?

2973. What flowers or herbs would you love to see growing in your perfect backyard?

2974. How long do you let your tea brew before it's just right for your taste?

2975. What symbol or story would you want to see engraved on a commemorative coin?

2976. How do you usually sleep, and what makes that position feel the most restful?

2977. What quirky or odd app do you remember stumbling on that made you laugh or cringe?

2978. What situation made you feel envious lately—and what did you learn from it?

2979. If a prize lasted forever, what product or perk would you want it to be?

2980. What would you do with a secret extra hour that nobody else had?

2981. If you were planning a picnic for stuffed animals, what would be on the menu?

2982. Did you ever knock something over in a store and end up having to replace it?

2983. What's one fear or thought you find hard to shake—even when others try to reassure you?

2984. Would your inner pup be more about play or skill—how many tennis balls would fit in your mouth?

2985. What was the most unexpected or intriguing subject you talked about recently?

2986. What serious or romantic film would instantly become a zombie spoof with one title twist?

2987. Can you solve one of those tricky cubes—and if yes, what's your proudest time?

2988. What moment or misstep required forgiveness—and what did you learn from it?

2989. If you had quadruplets, how would you pick names that connect or stand apart?

2990. What food do you think people around the world instantly associate with America?

2991. What's the most bizarre or interesting conversation you've had with a travel seatmate?

2992. What's a subject that seems to start disagreements in relationships or families?

2993. What word do you double-check every time because it just won't stick?

2994. What small or grand moment would feel perfect for a deeply romantic proposal?

2995. Who are three famous people you'd pick for a fun, silly game that breaks the ice?

2996. What did you once feel was part of your identity, but now you've outgrown it?

2997. If you feel in tune with things others don't notice, how would you describe that gift?

2998. What interaction recently left you needing to take a breath and process your feelings?

2999. When the sun is shining and the temperature feels ideal, how do you like to spend your time?

3000. Is there a popular tip or belief that you think is more harmful than helpful?

### Enjoy a Free Digital Copy of This Transformational Journal—My Gift to You

Thank you for showing up for yourself and taking this powerful step toward daily self-care, reflection, and personal growth.

As a heartfelt gift, I'm offering you a FREE digital copy of THIS IS MY WAY: 365 Positive Thoughts and Self-Care Journal.

It's packed with inspiring messages and thought-provoking questions to help you build confidence, reduce anxiety, and reconnect with what matters most —all year long.

Claim your free e-copy by scanning this QR code:

### Prefer a Physical Copy?

Many readers love having a physical copy to hold, highlight, or gift to someone special. If that sounds like you, you can grab your printed copy here:

Buy the hardcover version on Amazon by scanning this QR code:

Thank you for allowing me to be a small part of your self-care journey.

Here's to a year of reflection, growth, and positive change.

Aria Capri Publishing